ADVANCE PRAISE

"Travis and Angie from GSD Coach & Recruiting have been invaluable partners to SaaS Academy for several years, and their dedication and impact have been remarkable. From day one, Travis has been fully engaged with clients, the team, and other partners, consistently embodying a 'value-first' mindset. Whether teaching live calls, engaging in the community, or coaching clients through complex transitions, Travis always steps up to deliver. He has a unique ability to identify the specific needs of each client and guide them effectively, ensuring they're ready to benefit from his expertise. His hands-on approach, attention to detail, and genuine commitment to helping others have made him a trusted resource and a standout within the community. Both Travis and Angie are deeply involved in every aspect of the partnership, and their methodical approach to building, implementing, and scaling processes has been transformative for countless clients. *Doubling Down as DualPreneurs* is a testament to the skills and values they demonstrate every day."

–Johnny Page, CEO SaaS Academy &
Bestselling Author of *Software As A Science*

"I've had the pleasure of working with Travis & Angie through SaaS Academy, where they've helped us and many of our clients recruit world-class talent. They're a rare breed in that they are world-class operators with a successful track record, and have done so while maintaining the highest level of integrity and alignment to their values. If you're an aspiring entrepreneur, modeling these two and the fundamental lessons they share in this book is a sure bet."

–Marcel Petitpas, CEO Parakeeto & Bestselling Author

"I got to know Angie when our paths crossed in the Western Union Compliance Department. Angie, who at the time was a Project Manager, was curious about what we were *actually* doing. Her intense need to understand the subject matter and her enduring willingness to learn is what I think makes Angie so successful. She's a grafter and she is always full-in. Angie has an amazingly positive attitude she takes with her everywhere. Hard-working, smart, kind, and generous."

–Judith Trounson, Product Manager

"Imagine an extraordinarily efficient individual, one with a passion for team and process building, and filled with positive energy and a sharp focus on the task at hand. That's Angie Janko. The book she and Travis have authored offers insight into how you can take varied and extensive career experiences, marry them with a partner that complements each other's strengths, and provide practical lessons and frameworks for how to run a small business effectively, and efficiently, all while having fun. For those thinking of leaving the corporate world, who already have or have started their own business, this book brings a wealth of straightforward observations and learnings to all who read this book."
—Himanshu Niranjani, CTO Property Finder | Built Resilient Organizations at Microsoft, Amazon, Meta, LinkedIn | Angel Human-Capitalist, Startup Coach

"Angie develops deep relationships with her peers, colleagues, & direct reports and can quickly assess a challenge and develop a solution to achieve a favorable outcome. I always counted on Angie to be trustworthy, thoughtful, diligent, empathetic, and candid in her feedback and decision-making process. The book Angie and Travis have written will illustrate their use of open communication and a systematic, process-oriented approach to running their small businesses. A great read!"
—Jamar Freeze, Accredited Investor and Founder of multiple small businesses, including Freeze Strategic Initiatives, TrophyCoffee, FTW Ventures, and Dominanz Media Group

"Travis and Angie helped us land one of the best salespeople we could have found in a short period of time and with very little effort from my side. Their service is top notch and you can tell they've been doing this long enough to really know how to match people to organizations and "headhunt" with the best of them. I've also gotten to learn a lot from Travis by talking shop with him over the years and I appreciate what he knows and has taught me about ways to grow my business."
—Jeremiah Smith Founder and CEO of Simple Tiger

DOUBLING DOWN
AS
DUALPRENEURS

TRAVIS & ANGIE JANKO

DOUBLING DOWN
AS
DUALPRENEURS

Lessons from Living in and
LEAVING
the Corporate World

DOUBLING DOWN AS DUALPRENEURS
Lessons from Living in and Leaving the Corporate World

Copyright © 2025 by Travis and Angie Janko

All rights reserved. No part of this book may be reproduced, distributed, or transmitted in any form or by any means, including photocopying, recording, or other electronic or mechanical methods, without the written permission from the publisher or author, except as permitted by U.S. copyright law or in the case of brief quotations embodied in a book review.

Disclaimer: Although the publisher and the author have made every effort to ensure that the information in this book was correct at press time and while this publication is designed to provide accurate information in regard to the subject matter covered, the publisher and the author assume no responsibility for errors, inaccuracies, omissions, or any other inconsistencies herein and hereby disclaim any liability to any party for any loss, damage, or disruption caused by errors or omissions, whether such errors or omissions result from negligence, accident, or any other cause.

Interior Layout and Design by Stephanie Anderson
Jacket Design by Jess LaGreca

ISBNs:
979-8-89165-205-7 *Paperback*
979-8-89165-207-1 *Hardback*
979-8-89165-208-8 *E-book*

Published by:
Streamline Books
Kansas City, MO
streamlinebookspublishing.com

We dedicate this book to all those who dare to think outside the "corporate world" box and challenge themselves to "go big or go home." The journey of starting a business and nurturing its growth is challenging. Here's to those who aren't afraid to fail, pick themselves up, and try, try again. We believe in you! And we believe in ourselves!

CONTENTS

Introduction xi

PART ONE
OUR LEADERSHIP JOURNEY

1. Travis's Story 3
2. Angie's Story 15
3. Coming Together 27

PART TWO
OUR LEADERSHIP PHILOSOPHY

4. It's All About Relationships 37
5. Real Communication 49

PART THREE
TACTICAL TOOLS

6. Dumb Things to Avoid 69
7. Don't Chase Shiny Objects 83
8. Hiring Top Talent 95
9. The Power of Promotion 111
10. Ways of Working 119
11. Project Management 127
Conclusion 145

Acknowledgments 149
About the Authors 151
Endnotes 153

INTRODUCTION

IF YOU ARE AN ENTREPRENEUR or a business owner, you probably know the feeling of being overwhelmed—constantly busy but not necessarily always productive. Most entrepreneurs work long hours, sacrifice personal time, and still feel like progress eludes them.

Do you ever think, "No matter how hard I work, I just can't get my business to grow! I'm constantly busy, but I don't know what to focus on or what tasks to prioritize!" If so, we've been there. We understand the feeling, and we want to help.

This book chronicles our journey from being leaders in our respective corporate fields to becoming successful owners of two thriving businesses. We started with one business and, like most entrepreneurs, made many mistakes and struggled initially. However, through relentless learning and adaptation, we turned it into a seven-figure success. Using the same blueprint, we replicated our achievements with a second business, all without hiring any employees other than ourselves, leveraging nearly identical processes and tools to help the second business get off the ground quickly.

Our purpose in writing this book is to help you learn from our mistakes and successes. By the time you finish reading it, you will have plenty of key "aha!" moments and actionable takeaways to apply in your own business planning and execution process. We believe the formula we've developed works for any business, not just small startups or two-person teams.

The principles we used were initially honed during our employment at other companies where we created structure and processes for current-state gaps and revamped existing processes to make them streamlined, simple, and clear. We are big proponents of relentlessly improving operations.

When we started our first business, we overlooked some of these valuable lessons we'd learned from our corporate gigs and spent years figuring them out again. Now, we want to provide a playbook for those who are either starting out or feeling stuck so they can avoid our struggles and achieve success faster and more efficiently.

Along the way, we'll address common pitfalls, such as not differentiating between time spent and actual accomplishments. We'll discuss the stress, lack of sleep, and sometimes unhealthy behaviors that often accompany running a business. We aim to help you get out of that rut and find a more balanced approach to achieving your goals.

CONFRONTING THE CHAOS

In our daily interactions with business owners, we find that many feel a bit lost, and they often lack clear processes for essential aspects of their business. If you're in that same boat, this book can serve as a GPS, providing clear direction to guide you towards successfully obtaining your business goals. We promise to be brutally honest about our own missteps as we offer valuable insights—gold nuggets—that you can reinvest in your business to achieve significant growth.

INTRODUCTION

The entrepreneurial journey is fraught with many challenges. We empathize with anyone who feels like they are constantly dealing with chaos, running around with their hair on fire, and experiencing a new perceived crisis at every turn. Unfortunately, entrepreneurs often exacerbate their problems by failing to prioritize effectively, which can lead to randomization and eventual burnout. Before you reach that point, we're going to help you step back, teach you some tips on evaluating priorities, and enhance your effectiveness in annual and quarterly planning as well as day-to-day operations.

One common mistake small business owners make is hiring too many people too quickly because they think a larger team will help tackle the many challenges ahead. However, we're going to show you that it's possible to run a successful small business without expanding your team beyond your means. While some businesses, like a growing SaaS company, may require extensive staffing, others, like small consulting firms, often do not. We have operated two successful businesses with just the two of us simply by relying on efficient processes and clear boundaries as well as establishing successful partnerships with others who have expertise that we may not have.

Our journey from corporate leadership roles to successful business owners has been filled with valuable lessons and insights—some of them won through hard and relentless effort and constant innovation. We intend to share these with you so you can build a more efficient, productive, and ultimately successful business.

So let's start our journey together.

PART ONE
OUR LEADERSHIP JOURNEY

CHAPTER ONE

TRAVIS'S STORY

ACT NOW, ASK FOR FORGIVENESS LATER

I (TRAVIS) HAD BEEN IN leadership roles at large companies for years. The last "corporate" company I worked at was Hibu, Inc. In my three years there, the sales department almost quadrupled in size. During this time, we went from being a one-size-fits-all sales team to multiple specialized teams. It wasn't easy, and as you can imagine, there was a lot of pain and pushback as we made several important changes to our sales process.

Now, let me be clear up front. It was a great company to work for, and I met and worked alongside a lot of talented people. However, because it is in my nature to find "holes" or "gaps" in processes, I couldn't help but notice a few areas that needed improvement and optimization. The same would hold true for all of the companies I worked for during my years in the corporate world.

The first thing I noticed was the lack of specialization. Everyone on the team did everything, which meant no one could really focus on any specific task. Once we were able to try, test, and adjust multiple times, we turned the sales floor into a specialized machine. People began to see the value they brought to their work, and this was when the massive growth started.

Eventually, I left Hibu and took a sales leader position at Trulia, which was my first official startup. When I first started, I was supposed to receive six weeks of training. However, after only two weeks, my leader pulled me aside and said, "Congratulations, you now have a team." I was thrilled, but she quickly added that I had to start managing them *the next day!* The previous sales leader, who was loved by the team, had just been fired, and the team was underperforming. They only hit thirty-three percent of their quota the previous month.

To make matters worse, the team was known as the "Monkey in the Middle" because they were the lowest-performing team, and they were forced to sit in the middle of the floor for everyone to see—a kind of public humiliation intended to force better outcomes. If anything, it had the opposite effect. Additionally, two team members had applied for my role and were upset they didn't get it. All of this was a recipe for disaster, and I wondered if I had made a mistake taking this leadership role.

The first few days of leading the team were rough. On the first day, when I asked my leader who could build a couple of pitch decks for my sales team, she laughed and said, "If you need a thing done, you have to do that thing yourself." I was used to having support staff for such tasks, so this was a big adjustment. It was my big welcome and first eye-opening experience in the startup world.

At the same time, the top sales leaders on my team were unhappy about my presence, so I had to figure out how to win them over. I focused on understanding their needs and concerns, building trust, and showing them I was there to support them. It was a delicate balance, but I gradually turned the situation around and transformed a demoralized team into a cohesive and motivated unit.

TRAVIS'S STORY

I then turned my attention to a significant issue similar to one I saw at Hibu: There was no specialization among the sales staff at Trulia. Everyone was doing everything—cold calling, handling inbound leads, closing new business, managing accounts, and upselling. This lack of focus meant no one was excelling at anything. I decided to change that.

I approached my leader with the idea of creating specialized roles, only to be met with a blank stare and firm resistance. Every manager I pitched the idea to thought I was crazy. It was baffling to me, but I didn't give up. I began studying the top three salespeople in the company, spending hours observing their methods. I discovered that while the quotas were evenly split among new business, retention, and upselling, these top performers had found a way to game the system by focusing solely on their strengths.

Armed with this insight, I pitched the idea again, and I was given a small window to test things out. I gathered my team of nine and divided them based on their strengths. Those who excelled at acquiring new business focused solely on that while others concentrated on upselling or managing existing accounts. The transformation was immediate.

I began sharing my methods with other leaders. Within a month, my Monkey-in-the-Middle team became the number two sales team in the company. The following month, we hit 140 percent of our goal, with nearly everyone on the team topping the sales charts. By allowing my team to specialize, they exceeded their quotas, with some hitting 300 percent of their targets!

Despite our success, my approach raised eyebrows. Some of the upper management were concerned about breaking the established process, and I almost got written up for it. The leaders at Trulia were good people, but they were like so many others—set in their ways and clinging to the mantra, "This is how we've always done it." They often didn't know why they did things a certain way, but

DOUBLING DOWN AS DUALPRENEURS

they were determined to continue doing it, even if it bordered on the ridiculous.

I noticed this resistance intensifying as the company began to grow. People found their jobs becoming more uncomfortable as the company moved away from simple plug-and-play solutions.

Despite the initial pushback, I persisted in making changes. I wanted to build an account management team, which would essentially be an upsell team, from scratch. At first, my idea was shot down, but I went ahead and built a team anyway. They completely crushed it. The team started with a few members and grew to about thirty people. They regularly broke quotas, and in one quarter, they outperformed expectations for the entire year!

To be fair, I had cherry-picked the best leads, but my team's success was noticed. Naturally, after our triumph, management tripled our quotas and also pulled those great leads and gave them to the top sales people in the company instead. This led to some attrition among the team members, but I remained undeterred. I drew a line in the sand and committed to my approach.

Along the way, I learned the power of both innovation and persistence. I learned the importance of understanding a team's strengths and leveraging them for maximum impact. To do that, I had to challenge the status quo and find new ways to achieve success, even when faced with stiff resistance. I call it the "Act Now, Ask for Forgiveness Later" approach.

By the time I left Trulia, the company had grown from thirty-five to 600 employees, each working in their own specialized teams. There was an inbound team, an outbound team, an upsell team, and an account management team, all strategically positioned throughout the building.

With these specialized teams, the sales office became a well-oiled machine. New hires now spent up to a month in the training bay where trainers assessed their skills to determine the best team for them. This system worked so well that things just started rolling smoothly. The success story spread, and slowly but surely, the company began to embrace the idea of specialization.

I had played a vital role in creating these teams. I jumped from one team to another, much like a project manager, setting them up for success and then moving on to the next. This process-oriented approach contributed significantly to the company's success, which eventually led to an IPO and a $3.5 billion sale.

The key to my success at Trulia was building scalable processes and ensuring that every team member knew their specific role. This eliminated the inefficiencies of having employees try to juggle multiple tasks, thereby not excelling at anything.

TAKING MATTERS INTO MY OWN HANDS

A lack of specialization wasn't the only problem I faced at Trulia. The company's recruiting strategy focused on hiring for cultural fit, which often meant finding people who enjoyed casual office perks like keg parties, ping pong, and walking around barefoot. This approach frequently led to hiring mistakes.

I spent countless hours interviewing candidates who weren't suitable for the job, which took valuable time away from my team. Frustrated, I repeatedly met with the recruiting department to outline the specific profiles I needed, but despite their smiles and nods, nothing changed.

Realizing I had to take matters into my own hands, I trained myself to become a candidate-sourcing specialist. It wasn't my job, but I saw no other option. I would wake up at three or four in the morning to source candidates before work and continue during lunch breaks and after work.

DOUBLING DOWN AS DUALPRENEURS

My dedication paid off—out of the almost 600 people hired over the next three years, I personally found about 250 of them. This not only solved the hiring problem but also set a new standard for the recruiting department. This experience ignited my passion for recruiting.

When I moved to Fivestars, I was their very first Denver-based employee and faced the challenge of building everything from scratch. It was a rough-and-tumble experience. The power went out the first day, so I found myself assembling Ikea desks by flashlight and closing deals on my cell phone while also conducting interviews. However, we quickly outgrew our space, expanding to sixty people in about a year, and we eventually moved to a larger building where we grew to 120 people in just six additional months.

I hired three recruiting agencies, only to fire them after three weeks because they provided sub-par candidates. Once again, I took matters into my own hands, sourcing prospective employees early in the morning and late into the night.

A significant challenge arose when Facebook made changes to its advertising algorithm that we weren't planning for, which led to the worst month the company had seen in a long time. This crisis came just before our Series C funding round in which we raised $50 million.

The blame game began right away—marketing accused sales of not making enough calls while sales blamed marketing for poor leads. I knew these accusations were counterproductive, so my message to my team was to focus on what we knew was still working—the current pipeline. But some leadership didn't see it that way; they believed the issue came down to a lack of dials, so they wanted us to increase our call volume. And that's what we did.

Ironically, the top performers made the fewest calls but brought in the most revenue. Yet I was asked to reprimand them for not hitting their dial targets, a frustrating but necessary step to align with the new mandate.

This experience highlighted a common issue: When faced with a bad month, instead of analyzing and tweaking existing processes, people tend to panic and overhaul everything, which often makes things worse. I frequently had to remind my team not to change successful strategies due to a few bad days. After all, bad days are just opportunities to evaluate, adjust, and restart.

Eventually, all of the leaders jumped on board with this specialized approach, and we ultimately wound up selling the business for $317 million.

CHALLENGES IN LEADERSHIP TODAY

Overall, my time in corporate leadership revealed a critical issue: *the tone at the top*. At all three companies—Hibu, Trulia, and Fivestars—I encountered a few leaders who were unprepared for meetings or skipped them altogether. This behavior trickled down, with other managers emulating the same lack of preparation and commitment. True leaders should be on time, prepared, and treat every interaction with their direct reports as important. Unfortunately, that is not always the case.

Determined to set a better example, starting at Hibu, I created a one-page document for one-on-ones and weekly team leadership meetings that emphasized the importance of showing up on time and being prepared. Despite the shortcomings of some of the leaders around me, I maintained my commitment to these standards. This approach started to catch on, and other salespeople noticed. Those who appreciated real coaching wanted to join my team, while those who didn't like the accountability sought to leave, which helped ensure my team was filled with the right people.

My commitment to doing things the right way, even when my leaders didn't, eventually led to changes in my peers' behavior. During group meetings and one-on-ones, I would set the agenda and hold everyone accountable. Over time, this began to influence other leaders to follow suit.

At the same time, I learned the importance of being adaptable and resilient. When things didn't work, I had to get creative, find solutions, and push forward even in the face of fierce resistance. I developed a scrappy, hands-on approach, refusing to take no for an answer and rolling up my sleeves to fix problems. This approach became the foundation of Angie's and my success in both of our businesses.

Reflecting on that period in my career, I've identified several overarching challenges in leadership today.

First, one of the most significant issues is the **lack of scalable and repeatable processes**. Many companies tend to do a bunch of things at any given time without developing a structured approach, which leads to inconsistency and inefficiency. Even when a scalable and repeatable process is in place, it's often challenging to get people to follow it. And once a process is built, it *must* be re-evaluated and audited on a regular basis to ensure that it still makes sense and works well. You can't leave your processes on cruise control.

Second, there's a mentality of **"this is how we've always done it."** Many leaders struggle to step out of their comfort zones, so they stick to outdated methods even when they are no longer effective. I realized I had two choices: Join my peers in complaining about the system or take matters into my own hands and find a way to make things work. I chose the latter. I frequently encountered sales directors with innovative ideas who were stifled by rigid systems, and I encouraged them to find ways to safely test those ideas. The system won't change until someone presents a viable alternative.

TRAVIS'S STORY

A third major issue I observed was a **lack of trust from leadership**, particularly when it came to empowering employees. Leaders would hire top talent for their expertise and creativity, only to shackle them with restrictions that prevented them from truly making an impact. This lack of trust became more pronounced with the rise of remote work where leaders couldn't see employees' efforts firsthand and doubted their productivity.

This mistrust creates a toxic environment. Employees feel undervalued and micromanaged while employers struggle to let go of outdated management styles. The tension leads to frustration on both sides. Employees, confident in their abilities, feel constrained by a lack of autonomy while employers are reluctant to loosen the reins.

This environment of mistrust and micromanagement stifles creativity and progress. Leaders often fear that if their subordinates outshine them, they might lose their positions or promotions, so they are reluctant to allow employees the freedom to innovate. Additionally, some leaders are afraid that empowering their teams might expose their own lack of productivity. Many leaders maintain the status quo with minimal effort, which makes them uncomfortable with someone coming in with new ideas that could require more work.

Ultimately, I believe our success in business stems from Angie and me being willing to fully trust each other and allow for creativity and innovation. We don't have anyone dictating how to run our businesses, and we trust in our methods and each other's abilities.

DOUBLING DOWN AS DUALPRENEURS

STEPPING OUT OF THE CORPORATE WORLD

Eventually, frustration and a vision for something greater drove me out of the corporate leadership world. I found myself constantly swimming upstream in the corporate environment, repeatedly hitting an invisible wall that stifled my progress. I couldn't understand why these barriers existed. My belief was simple: If you want to keep moving forward and have the ability to do so, you should at least have the chance to keep swimming. If you're in corporate leadership, you can probably relate to that feeling.

My frustrations grew as I realized the significant impact I was making in these companies. I was helping my managers succeed by teaching them several key leadership principles. It became clear that I could do this on my own and be successful. In fact, I could do even better without the constraints of corporate life.

Throughout my corporate career, I had a knack for coaching and managing up. By presenting my coaching as advice, I became a trusted advisor, subtly guiding senior leadership without them realizing it. At the same time, many of my peers succeeded because they also started following the playbooks and processes I helped build.

This coaching experience made me realize I could apply the same principles to my own business. I could help others grow and improve professionally, and it would be far more rewarding to do this for my own clients than for a corporate entity. But everything I read and heard suggested that starting my own business would be nearly impossible. I was scared it might not work, so I started the business while still working full time for another company. This dual approach provided a safety net: If the business failed, I still had my job.

However, I quickly realized this was a terrible outlook because it was based on a mindset of scarcity and fear rather than one of abundance and success. Instead, I set a more ambitious goal: Once my business generated more income than my corporate salary, I would go all in. This mindset change made a big difference in my approach, and it wasn't long before I had the conversation with my corporate boss: "I can't afford to work here any longer."

Many potential entrepreneurs face the same fear. They're afraid of stepping out on their own and leaving the safety of the corporate world. Fear of failure is common, but there's also a fear of what their inner circle will think. They worry about whether their friends, family, and peers will support them or be OK with the long hours and the risk involved. In reality, those are the very people they shouldn't be trying to please. Often, it's better to find a new inner circle that supports their entrepreneurial ambitions.

Moreover, some people are not just afraid of failure—they're afraid of success. They think, "What if I do really well, and I'm not prepared for it? What happens then?" These fears are natural, but overcoming them is part of the journey. If anything, Angie's and my story is a testament to the power of pushing past these fears, embracing abundance, and trusting in our own abilities to build something greater on our own terms.

LESSONS LEARNED

One of the most valuable skills I developed in corporate leadership was the ability to stay open-minded and flexible. Remembering to breathe, closing my eyes and just taking a deep breath, got me through a lot of tough and frustrating moments. There were countless times when I felt great about how things were progressing, only to walk into the office the next day and find that everything was shifting in a bad direction. This was often due to what I call "shiny object syndrome," a common affliction in many companies.

DOUBLING DOWN AS DUALPRENEURS

Shiny object syndrome is when a company gets distracted by the latest trend or idea. Maybe someone attended a conference, read a book, watched a movie, or had a conversation that sparked the idea of making sweeping changes. Even if the current strategy is working, the allure of something new and untested can derail the focus. This happens *constantly* in the corporate world, and it's a huge hindrance.

You must resist the shiny objects and stay focused on what works. Do not be swayed by every new idea that comes along. Embracing flexibility doesn't mean chasing every trend; it means being adaptable while staying grounded in proven strategies and maintaining a laser focus on the business goals.

This lesson has been a guiding principle for me in building our businesses. While innovation is fully welcome, it must be approached with a balanced and thoughtful mindset. Realizing this has enabled Angie and me to create and grow two successful businesses with absolutely no employees!

CHAPTER TWO

ANGIE'S STORY

CAREER VAGABOND

I (ANGIE) NEVER SET OUT to be a career vagabond, meandering from company to company and industry to industry, but I'm thankful for what it has taught me. I've seen the challenges that are widespread in the business world, and I've gained the ability to assess situations and recommend solutions using a diverse set of tools and strategies. More than that, all of these varied experiences set the stage for me to hone my listening, process improvement, project management, and consulting skills, which led to the birth of my business, Done! LLC.

Along the way, I've worked hard to build a foundation based on honest curiosity and a deep passion for learning. I am constantly trying to identify opportunities for improvement—whether they relate to people, processes, or tools—collaborate with others to evaluate potential solutions, and then implement those solutions to the point where they can be handed off as business as usual.

Once that's done, I always find myself asking, "What's next?" And if the organization I'm working with doesn't have an answer to that question—if they don't have any more problems for me to solve or new roles for me to take on—I move on to the next company that has a big problem to solve.

This dynamic has defined my entire career. I guess you could say I'm a firm believer in automating processes and working myself out of a job so I can move on to help someone else.

No task is too small for me. I'm as comfortable handling administrative duties as I am tackling large-scale global enterprise initiatives. I adapt my communication and working styles to fit the needs of those around me because I've learned that relationships are everything in the business world. Success most often comes from making others successful, and I genuinely love working with people to solve problems. Yes, it can be challenging at times, but it's also a lot of fun.

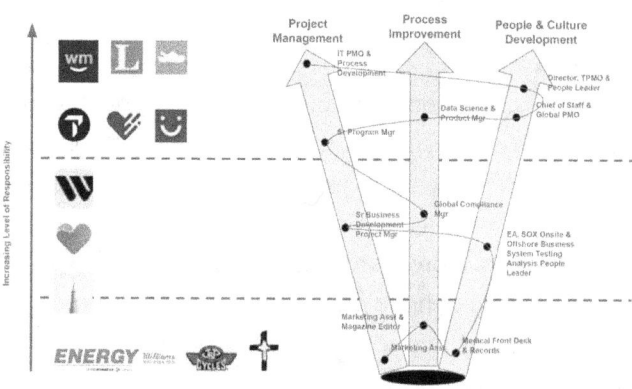

FIGURE 1

A DIVERSE TRAJECTORY

A relatively brief overview of my corporate career will give you some idea of the diverse range of experiences I've had over the years (see Figure 1) and how it enabled me to become a successful

ANGIE'S STORY

project management consultant for both small businesses and larger enterprises.

After college, I began working as a sales rep for MetLife selling life insurance and annuities. While I enjoyed helping people get their affairs in order, I quickly realized that a career in sales wasn't for me. However, I learned that sales is a component of every job, so I've woven that skill into my career alongside process improvement, project management, and people management.

After MetLife, I moved to Energy Manufacturing, where I worked as a marketing specialist. I loved the role because it allowed me to go out on the manufacturing floor and see how hydraulic pumps and cylinders were made for the agricultural industry. One of the most important lessons I learned there was that everyone, regardless of their role or title, deserves respect. Whether they're a janitor, a press operator on the manufacturing floor, or a VP in marketing, every person has an opinion and should be treated with dignity.

I was fortunate to work with people who treated me with respect and trust, which inspired me to do the same for others. One of my first big assignments in that role was redesigning the company logo, a design they're still using forty years later.

Later, I moved to J&P Cycles and began working in the aftermarket motorcycle parts industry—a world I had no prior experience in. Shortly after joining, the owner asked me if I'd be the editor of *Harley Women Magazine*, a publication he was considering purchasing. Despite my lack of knowledge about motorcycles or even the publishing industry, I agreed.

To get up to speed, I immersed myself in motorcycle culture by attending events like Sturgis and Daytona Bike Week and even getting my motorcycle license. My approach to learning is very hands-on, and this experience taught me not to be afraid of jumping into something new, embracing the possibility of failure, and learning along the way.

That job was a lot of fun, probably the most interesting role I've had in my career. However, after getting the magazine up and running and reselling it nine months later, I was ready for a change. I decided to move in a completely different direction, so I entered the healthcare industry.

Originally, I had gone to college with the intention of becoming a nurse and helping others, but during my second year of nursing school, the clinicals and the sight of blood got to me, and I realized I wasn't cut out for it—at least, not in a direct patient care perspective. However, I knew my skills with communication, organization, and a care for others would allow me to be successful in the healthcare industry.

I took a job at Mercy Hospital as a medical records assistant where I mostly avoided the blood and gore. During that time, I learned how to handle a wide variety of customer-facing situations since I was stationed at the front desk. Many people who come into a hospital are not in good spirits—they're ill, upset, and in pain. I had to learn to put on my empathy hat, figure out how to help them and make them comfortable, and stay calm.

After that, I moved to Aegon NV, a Dutch company that was later acquired and became Transamerica. This was where I spent the longest stint of my career and where I caught the "consulting bug." It's also where I *really* began my career vagabond trajectory.

I started as an executive assistant in the investment division, learning everything I could about funding and investment deals. I became very proficient in keeping information organized and ensuring we were in financial compliance in collaboration with our attorney and portfolio managers. This eventually led to increasingly higher-level promotions, which was a lot of fun as I was able to move from division to division and really get a feel for how the company operated from a holistic perspective. And, as you might imagine, I got to help them solve a lot of problems and establish processes to make our tasks run smoothly.

One of the biggest challenges I tackled was being a project manager for the Sarbanes-Oxley (SOX) efforts in North America. SOX compliance is incredibly important for financial companies in order to ensure their funds are being accounted for correctly using rigorous general computer control (GCC) IT requirements.

I spent a long time in this role until I reached a point where I asked, "What's next?" When there wasn't anything new for me to take on, I decided to move on.

I transitioned back into the medical field with a role at Denver Health. One of the most rewarding aspects of working at Denver Health was serving as a business development project manager where my job was to find new ways for the hospital to generate revenue.

My proudest achievement there was collaborating with hospital administration, physicians, nurses, clinical staff, and an outside healthcare partner, Kaiser Permanente, to resurrect the Electroconvulsive Therapy (ECT) program. ECT is used for patients with severe depression and mental disorders, but many mental healthcare facilities weren't offering it as an option to their patients. However, we recognized the benefits of reintroducing this service, and bringing it back proved to be a major success. The program not only benefited patients but also generated over a million dollars in revenue for the hospital within its first year. It was incredibly rewarding to be a part of such a meaningful project.

After my time at Denver Health, I moved on to Western Union where I took on a different kind of challenge. Western Union, as a global money transfer business, has to adhere to strict financial and legal compliance regulations to prevent issues like money laundering. One of the most important projects I undertook there was setting up an anti-human-trafficking program.

DOUBLING DOWN AS DUALPRENEURS

I collaborated closely with our legal counsel as well as state and federal officials to create an internal training program for Western Union agents as well as set up rule-based IT algorithms to flag suspicious wire transfer activities. This program aimed to identify and prevent the misuse of money transfer services by individuals involved in human trafficking.

We also launched a state-level promotional campaign to raise awareness about the issue. This experience opened my eyes to a side of the world I hadn't previously been exposed to, and it was both challenging and fulfilling.

Following my time at Western Union, I was recruited by Travelport to lead the implementation of a new global program management planning and delivery process, Scaled Agile Framework (SAFe). Travelport had been using Agile Scrum for software development and wanted to mature their processes by moving to Scaled Agile.

My work involved coordinating a massive program release train, which required aligning ten different teams across the U.S., England, and India, all working on various pieces of the project. I had to ensure that all of these teams were synchronized horizontally, which meant they had to understand the sequence of work, dependencies, and potential blockers. Once the system was up and running and the teams were operational, my role was complete, and I moved on to the next opportunity.

That next opportunity was at Healthgrades, a company that operates at the intersection of healthcare and consumer technology. Healthgrades offers a platform where consumers can search for doctors based on location and symptoms while physicians pay to appear in the search results and provide content for the site.

Initially, I was tasked with setting up a project management practice within their data science department. After successfully establishing the practice, I was asked by the CTO to step into a product manager role where I took charge of a foundering mobile app.

ANGIE'S STORY

I worked closely with our offshore engineering and design teams as we reimagined and relaunched the app using a new project management framework, Dual Track Scrum. This framework allowed our UI/UX and design teams to work two-to-four weeks ahead of the engineering team, ensuring the right work was ready at the right times. The result was a smooth and efficient flywheel effect for the mobile app's feature delivery.

Though I had never served as a product manager before, I threw myself completely into the role, devouring books, attending webinars, and learning from successful product managers, both within the company as well as from my external network. This relentless pursuit of knowledge and adaptability led to my success in that role.

Following my time at Healthgrades, I was recruited to join Visible, a startup within the Verizon family. Verizon tasked us with creating an all-digital telecom company, and that's exactly what we did. We launched a completely online phone service that offered month-to-month plans specifically designed to be affordable and accessible for people with lower incomes or those who were less tech-savvy.

The CTO of Visible then asked me to step into the role of his Chief of Staff where I oversaw a $40 million budget and managed nine teams spread across the globe. We worked diligently to streamline our engineering practices and organizational structure, bringing much-needed clarity to roles. I was also selected from over 7,500 global applicants to be part of the Women of the World Leadership program, which was a highlight of my time at Visible.

Recently, a project I worked on at Visible bore fruit when the company was granted a patent for a "risk assessment and resolution for end device porting and activation" process. This process and algorithm that I helped develop identifies users who are having trouble completing an onboarding procedure when they move their phone (and number) from one mobile carrier to another.

DOUBLING DOWN AS DUALPRENEURS

The service calculates the onboarding risk value in order to identify users who are having difficulty. It also calculates the onboarding risk value based on a set of criteria pertaining to an incomplete onboarding process. It then performs remedial steps to correct the onboarding errors and facilitates a successful completion of the porting process.

This may sound fairly complex, but in essence, it's intended to help users of mobile devices who want to change their wireless service provider but keep their current telephone number. This is a common and extremely frustrating experience for many people, and the now-patented process provides a solution. A definite win-win for the customers and the company! I was involved with four team members on developing this service during my time at Visible, so it's nice to see them finally receive a patent for it, too.

In the later stages of my corporate career, I took on roles at WM Technology (Weedmaps), a canna-tech platform, and Lakeshore, an educational materials and supply institution. In both positions, I served as a director and focused on setting up their project management offices. My efforts were aimed at building robust processes, ensuring clear understanding of roles and responsibilities, and helping these organizations transition into the twenty-first century from a project management perspective.

My final corporate role was at Crocs where I decided to step back from leadership and focus on being an individual contributor. I was brought in to lead their program management practice for the Crocs portfolio within the IT division, but during my sixteen months there, the company went through several restructures. This period of transition was a turning point for me, and it was then that Travis and I realized it was time to focus on growing our own businesses. After years of improving processes, managing people, and refining tools for others, it felt right to direct that energy toward our ventures. I was rejuvenated and excited for this decision.

ANGIE'S STORY

THE PATTERNS I'VE OBSERVED

Thanks to a wide range of experiences, I was able to help many different companies get on solid footing with stronger and more efficient processes. In fact, I attribute much of my success to my career-vagabond approach. As it turns out, with solid skill sets in project management, process development, and tool evaluation and implementation, a genuine passion for my work, and a love for people, it didn't matter what industry I was in or the job title I held. The key was to stay naturally curious and always look for ways to help others succeed.

Along the way, I learned a few important things about myself. First, I **always dive in 100 percent**, learning the product, company, and culture from the outset. Unlike many who gradually acclimate, I immerse myself fully right from the start, and I tend to retain a great number of details from years past.

Second, I always **look for ways to make even the most mundane tasks engaging**, an approach that not only helped me gain buy-in from my teams but also enabled me to navigate the frequent restructurings that seemed to follow me at every company I joined. In fact, reorganizations are so common in the corporate world that they are practically a quarterly ritual at some companies.

Many leaders are quick to restructure as their first response to challenges without **first considering whether a simple process change might solve the problem**. This tendency to reorganize often overlooks the root causes of issues and isn't always the most effective solution. In addition, frequent restructurings are incredibly challenging for employees and contribute to high turnover and a feeling of exhaustion.

Another lesson I learned through my extensive experience in project management is that a one-size-fits-all approach just doesn't work. Early in my career, I thought I could create a standard template for setting up project management office processes and structures in any organization, but I quickly discovered that each company is unique. **The success of a project management office (PMO) depends on understanding the specific needs of the company as well as the values of its leaders.**

Now I approach setting up a project management office with a much more tailored mindset. I start by identifying the pain points and challenges the company is facing. If the primary issue is a lack of visibility into projects or financial spending, then the PMO's value might lie in providing robust reporting. On the other hand, if the problem is that work doesn't align with strategic initiatives, the PMO might need to focus on governance and portfolio management as well as enforcing stricter controls over project prioritization, selection, and funding.

You can't impose a project management structure on an organization without first understanding its unique needs. Once those needs are identified, the PMO can be designed to deliver the greatest benefit. Furthermore, leaders must continually communicate the PMO's value to the organization in order to ensure that its purpose and impact are clearly understood. Without ongoing communication, the value of project management might be questioned, which can lead others to feel disengaged from or dissatisfied with the PMO.

THE VALUE OF BEING A CONSULTANT

As a result of my diverse experiences across multiple industries, I developed a knack for entering a company, taking a step back, and assessing the entire landscape before making suggestions. Often, these suggestions weren't acted upon right away, largely because I was new to the company. However, almost without fail, I found

ANGIE'S STORY

myself hearing the same ideas being proposed by others later on down the road. Suddenly, a leader would share an idea that I had originally suggested during my first few weeks.

Interestingly, this scenario seemed to change when I stepped into the role of consultant. Right away, there was a noticeable difference in how my recommendations were received when I started being viewed as an external expert. A good example is when an international company brought me in to assist with a multi-phased Agile transformation for their software development, product, and go-to-market teams.

I began with a listening tour in which I heard more than fifty individuals at all levels of the organization explain what was working well and what wasn't. Based on these conversations, I compiled a report outlining my observations, identifying gaps, and recommending next steps. To my surprise, the company accepted my recommendations, and over the course of nine months, they implemented my suggestions and experienced noticeable improvements in the quality and cadence of their planning and delivery.

This phenomenon isn't unique to my experience. It seems that the title of consultant carries a certain weight that being an internal full-time employee does not. There's something about the perceived expertise of an external consultant that makes organizations more receptive to advice, even if the same advice has been offered internally for years without being acted upon. It's a curious dynamic, but it highlights how people respond differently to input depending on the source.

Stepping into the role of consultant not only changed business leaders' perception of me, but it also brought a significant change to my own demeanor. During my corporate years, as someone who generally avoids heated arguments and aggressive confrontation, I often found myself being more soft-spoken and less assertive in my recommendations. This lack of confidence sometimes prevented me from fully pushing my ideas forward.

To overcome this limitation, I would often review Figure 2[1] to remind myself to keep pushing for growth and new opportunities. Even now, Travis and I use this graphic within our businesses to make sure we keep challenging ourselves to step out of our comfort zones.

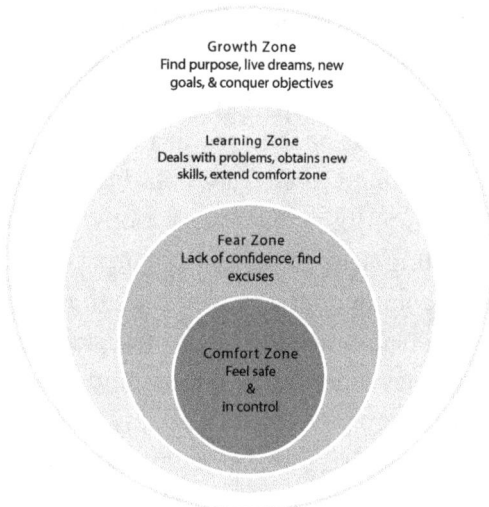

FIGURE 2

As a consultant, my business and reputation are on the line, and with decades of experience under my belt, I'm more assertive, confident, and direct than ever before. I know my expertise is valuable, and I've been hired for a reason. This shift in mindset—knowing I have the freedom and authority to drive results—allows me to approach my work now with a level of conviction that I didn't always feel as an employee. And that has made all the difference!

CHAPTER THREE
COMING TOGETHER

SO HOW DID WE FINALLY come together to form our elite dynamic duo of complementary skills?

During my years in the corporate world, I (Angie) would periodically help with the first business, GSD Coach & Recruiting, doing simple tasks like organizing documents or following up on specific actions. What started as a two-hour-a-week effort, fitting in the extra work during early mornings, evenings, or weekends, gradually evolved into something much more significant. Over time, as we collaborated, it became clear that we needed to take a closer look at the entire business process and each of our roles.

I took the initiative to document our standard operating procedures and create a Visio flowchart to map out the business process from start to finish. Through this detailed analysis, we identified significant gaps, redundancies, and inefficiencies within our operations. This led to many discussions about how I could further contribute. So we experimented with different steps in the process, finding areas where I could step in, even though not everything was a perfect fit initially.

DOUBLING DOWN AS DUALPRENEURS

As our partnership grew, I took on more responsibilities, particularly related to project management and client account management. I began handling our social media accounts, managing accounts payable and receivable, overseeing our books, and attending trade shows to promote the business.

By the time I started working at Crocs, my workload at GSD Coach & Recruiting had increased to the point that I was effectively juggling multiple jobs. At that point, I decided to commit full time to GSD.

Thus, a powerhouse "dualpreneurship" was truly born.

LEARNING OUR OWN LESSONS

In the beginning, I (Travis) mostly worked on a contract basis as a fractional VP of Sales for small startups. These were generally companies where the founders had developed a product that people were buying, but they lacked expertise in leadership and sales. My role was to help them build out their sales processes and structures.

As part of that work, I would also assist in hiring salespeople, a service I included without additional charge. I soon learned that I was particularly adept at recruiting and placing candidates, so I pivoted the business more toward full-time recruiting.

However, I was often overwhelmed with stress and long hours. I found myself bogged down by countless tasks, and I held the mistaken notion that as a business owner, I should handle everything myself. This is a common problem for entrepreneurs. So many business owners get caught up in countless tasks instead of focusing on what truly matters and where they excel.

Fortunately, once Angie got involved, we eventually discovered how to leverage our respective strengths. We each excel in different areas of the business, and we now allow each other to focus on the things we're each best suited for. Through open communication and mutual respect, we are able to stay aligned, and as a result, we have avoided many common pitfalls in business management. In fact, this dynamic of mutual understanding and effective communication has been foundationally important to the growth and health of our business, and we believe it distinguishes our approach from the often-flawed communication practices seen in other companies.

Because we were both working from home, we had to navigate both personal and professional boundaries more carefully. The elimination of long commutes meant we found ourselves with a lot of additional time, which we used to improve our physical and mental health by incorporating morning routines, exercise, and shared breakfasts into our day.

We also spent some time addressing inefficiencies and streamlining our processes. What started as a series of incremental realizations about the need for better organization and clearer role definitions gradually evolved into a more deliberate and structured approach to working together.

SCRUTINIZING EVERYTHING

We scrutinized every aspect of our operations, using comprehensive whiteboarding sessions to list and evaluate every task and responsibility in our business. This exhaustive process revealed some tasks we had been undertaking without fully realizing their necessity or impact. We categorized these tasks into three groups: mission critical, important but not urgent, and unnecessary.

We then analyzed what each of us excelled at and enjoyed versus what we didn't. This insight led to a clearer division of roles as we each turned our attention to our strengths and interests.

DOUBLING DOWN AS DUALPRENEURS

Despite this clarity, the transition wasn't immediate or easy. Even with defined roles, there were challenges in letting go of certain tasks and respecting the established boundaries. We frequently encountered situations where one of us might inadvertently step into the other's area of responsibility, which required ongoing, open communication to resolve.

As we continued refining our business processes, we realized that our daily activities were scattered and inefficient. We were constantly jumping from one task to another, which created a disjointed and stressful workday. To address this, we implemented time blocking, a technique that designates specific days for similar tasks.

For example, we set aside Mondays and Wednesdays for screening sales professionals for client roles. We decided that Tuesdays and Thursdays should be focused solely on client engagement and development. And we reserved Fridays to focus on planning and process improvement. This approach allowed us to become more proficient and focused, rather than spreading our efforts thin across various tasks throughout the week.

Additionally, because we were working excessively long hours, we looked for ways to cut down our work time significantly by boosting our efficiency. We began to prioritize our most important tasks early in the morning, leveraging our peak energy levels, and wrapped up our work by mid-afternoon. After a set time, typically around four o'clock in the afternoon, we stopped responding to business calls, texts, and emails to ensure that our personal time remained undisturbed. We made sure to communicate these boundaries to our clients to set clear expectations about our availability.

Another significant challenge was the disorganization of our documents. We had accumulated thousands of electronic files, and they were scattered across various folders, which made it nearly impossible to find what we needed quickly. To solve this problem, we undertook a massive and comprehensive reorganization of our Google Drive. We categorized documents into specific folders for training materials, public relations, social media, clients, and legal contracts. This overhaul created a more structured and accessible system and turned our previously chaotic file storage into an organized repository.

We also learned an important lesson about managing our time related to meetings. Early on, we would agree to meet with anyone who reached out to us, even if those individuals were not a good fit for our needs. Sometimes, we even took meetings with candidates who were looking for roles we didn't have or who were not the right type of candidate. Our intention was to be helpful, but it often led to wasted time for both parties.

So we became more protective of our time and began engaging only with those who could either benefit from our services or offer something in return. Casual conversations still happened, of course, but there were fewer of them. We made sure the bulk of our time was spent on more productive interactions.

When it came to setting and meeting financial goals, I (Travis) was the math nerd, so I took on the task of breaking down our revenue targets into manageable components. We would start by setting a large annual income goal, and then I would reverse engineer it to determine the number of deals needed based on our average deal size. This approach allowed us to focus on daily tasks and conversations that would lead to achieving our yearly target.

We used a whiteboard to visualize our goals and pacing—that was Angie's strength—and we adjusted our strategies as needed. By focusing on the process rather than the financial outcome, we were able to systematically reach our targets and even improve on them over time.

That was the point when it became clear to us that we needed to focus solely on our business rather than splitting our efforts with other jobs. Fortunately, we had reached a key financial milestone because our business was now generating more income than our other jobs (and requiring fewer hours).

To prevent our work together from taking over our relationship, we carefully separated our personal and professional lives. We established a routine in which our early mornings were dedicated to personal time rather than work. That way, we started our days with activities that focused on our well-being, things like reading, cooking breakfast together, playing cards, watching the news, and engaging in exercise like yoga, weightlifting, and walking. This gave us time for personal connection before the workday began, although it was often challenging to keep work topics at bay.

Additionally, we made sure to block off lunch nearly every day, which ensures that we avoid the all-too-common problem of skipping meals due to work demands. By reserving this time and stepping away from our computers, we maintain a healthy balance between work and personal life throughout the day. We also began scheduling monthly lunch dates at restaurants so we could physically step away from our work environment to reconnect.

We found it was also important to incorporate short, regular breaks into our routine. Most people experience a lull in the afternoon, but we deal with this by taking a short walk around the park in our neighborhood to refresh and rejuvenate.

And we planned vacations that allowed us the flexibility to get some work done if needed. For example, during a recent trip to Kauai, we cleverly took advantage of the four-hour time difference by working early in the morning. We got up at three o'clock in the morning and finished work by eight so we could enjoy the majority of our days at the beach without missing any work.

To maintain boundaries, we started having check-in meetings every day where we discussed what needed to be accomplished and who was responsible for each task. This kept us focused and organized, helped us avoid stepping on each other's toes, reminded us of the most important tasks to tackle, and allowed us to provide each other support as needed.

THE CHALLENGES OF RUNNING A SECOND BUSINESS

Launching, maintaining, and growing one business is hard enough, but we're now running two businesses, both Done! LLC and GSD Coach & Recruiting, at the same time. That might sound close to impossible, and we'll be honest with you—it is challenging. But you can make it work if you adopt the right approach.

Balancing our businesses requires a clear and careful division of time. On our whiteboard, we've delineated our schedule so that we're working on one business at a certain time of the day or day of the week and then shifting focus to our other business during the remaining time. This structured approach helps us manage our time effectively and maintain a balance between our professional commitments for each business.

The growth and success of our two businesses is closely tied to how we leverage each other's strengths and maintain a clear division of duties. In our collaborative roles, we act as guides and consultants to one another. This mutual support extends to both businesses, with each of us providing valuable insights and recommendations.

And we are constantly nurturing and growing our network. In fact, we believe much of our success is linked to our commitment to attending certain conferences where we are the exclusive recruiting partner. We regularly set up booths at these conferences and proactively engage with attendees, learning about their needs and sharing information about our services. Additionally,

DOUBLING DOWN AS DUALPRENEURS

I (Travis) participate in webinars, podcasts, and other training events throughout the year, contributing my expertise to a broader community and further establishing our presence in the industry.

Each of us brings very different but very valuable experiences to the table. It has been interesting to see how our skills naturally intertwine. Angie excels in customer-facing roles in which she develops trusting relationships and ensures that processes run smoothly. Travis, on the other hand, is more technical and has a keen eye for sourcing the right talent for specific roles.

We believe our story demonstrates that when people work together in harmony, filling in each other's gaps, it creates a powerful dynamic. So many companies have competitive environments where individuals work in silos rather than collaboratively, but our experience proves the value of recognizing and nurturing complementary skills to achieve greater success. When you come together, committed to shared success, you achieve far more than you ever thought possible!

Now, you may be thinking, *I don't need to know how to run two businesses. I just need to know how to get one business off the ground and make it profitable.* Fair enough. We're here to help. Over the next few chapters, we're going to share some actionable tips, tactics, and strategies that we've gleaned from our combined years of experience, both in our own businesses and in working with many clients across a wide range of industries.

PART TWO
OUR LEADERSHIP PHILOSOPHY

CHAPTER FOUR

IT'S ALL ABOUT RELATIONSHIPS

AT THE HEART OF ANY successful business lies one fundamental truth: It's all about relationships. Nurturing the human side of your business, whether through partnerships, team-building, or connections with peers and leaders, is what keeps things moving forward. Far too often, we encounter people in business who are overly focused on what's in it for them. They're consumed by thoughts like, "Why didn't I get this opportunity? Why isn't it fair?" This mindset overlooks the true power behind lasting success—relationships.

Throughout our careers, we've learned (and relearned) the importance of building strong, trusting relationships at every level. First, there's the team—the people we manage. Then, there are our peers, and finally, the leaders we report to. Each of these requires a different approach, but the foundation remains the same: creating a safe space where open, honest conversations are allowed and even welcomed.

When we started GSD, we invested a lot of time and energy into forming strong relationships with solid partners because we knew these partnerships would be key to our growth. And indeed, they have been.

It's important to note that when we say "partners," we're not just talking about clients. We're talking about anyone who plays a role in the success of our business. Some partners refer business to us while others help us complete a project. For example, we may collaborate with a recruiter when our bandwidth is stretched or make a referral when a client offers us a role that falls outside our expertise. These partnerships allow us to say yes to opportunities we might otherwise turn down.

But it's not enough to form these partnerships—we have to nurture them. If we aren't constantly staying connected with and doing everything we can to support our partners, we know we won't stay top of mind. And when we're not top of mind, those valuable referrals stop flowing.

So one of the principles we live by is this: Whenever we finish a transaction, a meeting, or even just a conversation, our goal is to leave the other person with something more than they had before. It isn't about closing a deal; it's about building a relationship and adding value.

For example, at the time of this writing, we have a meeting scheduled with someone who wants to be a potential referral partner. This individual is a fractional VP of sales, as I (Travis) used to be, so he helps companies develop their sales processes and playbooks. He reached out to us after hearing one of our podcasts, and now he's interested in exploring a partnership.

However, our primary goal in the upcoming conversation isn't to push for a partnership or to secure a deal. Instead, it's to learn more about this individual, build a relationship, and hopefully leave him with something useful he can take away from the meeting. We're not expecting anything in return because we believe that when you give without expectation, good things tend to come around naturally.

IT'S ALL ABOUT RELATIONSHIPS

In our experience, this approach works in every aspect of life. Recently, we met up with one of our teams of partners and contributors when we were all in Denver. We didn't have any agenda other than to connect, take a few photos, and enjoy some time together. It wasn't about what we could gain from the experience or what we could ask them to do. Rather, it was simply about doing something meaningful. People remember those types of moments.

In all honesty, we probably do more free consulting and coaching than we do paid work. And we're perfectly fine with that. Even when we're not giving away free advice, we are often spending time simply chatting with people. Potential clients often reach out to us just to touch base. They don't need anything from us at the moment, but they value the relationship. And they know they may need something from us in the future, so they want to stay in regular contact.

A lot of people would decline those meetings because they see them as a waste of time—there's no immediate opportunity on the table, no pressing need to fill. But we take them, and here's why: We've learned that even when there's no business on the horizon, there's almost always something valuable to gain.

Maybe we'll make a new connection. Maybe we'll help the potential client in some small way, which will keep us top of mind. And maybe—just maybe—that meeting will turn into something more down the road.

But even if it doesn't, that's fine. Remember, it's not about closing a deal every time. It's about building relationships and providing value. Every meeting doesn't have to be transactional. Sometimes, the payoff comes much later, and sometimes it doesn't come at all. But we still walk away knowing we've added something to the conversation, and often, the potential client walks away having given us something valuable too.

DOUBLING DOWN AS DUALPRENEURS

We also believe it's important to be OK with people not always giving back. Too often, interactions are transactional. People think, "What can I get out of this?" instead of focusing on the opportunity to offer something of value. That's why we like to give without expecting anything in return. If we do ask for help and it doesn't come, it can feel like a letdown. But even then, it's not a failure—it's something to reflect on and improve.

That being said, we don't take *every* meeting that comes our way. There has to be at least the *potential* for mutual benefit. By this, we don't mean that we expect a deal or immediate business to come from every interaction. Rather, we mean that there has to be some potential for each party to offer the other something meaningful, whether it's a new perspective, a helpful introduction, or a piece of advice that can make a difference. If we don't think this is likely, then it probably isn't worth the time for either party.

In our experience, the relationships we've cultivated and the value we've provided always come full circle in one way or another. Whether through business partnerships, team dynamics, or personal interactions, we always strive to add something meaningful to the lives of others. In doing so, we not only enrich their experience, but we also build a foundation of trust, goodwill, and mutual success.

Now, here's the tricky part. Sometimes, people would gladly reciprocate if they knew how to return the value in some way. One day, I (Travis) spoke with Dan Martel, author of *Buy Back Your Time* (a great book packed with valuable insights, by the way). We had a twenty-minute recorded conversation where I asked him questions, and he provided his perspective. After the recording, I asked, "Is there anything you think I should change about myself?"

Without hesitation, Dan said, "Yes. You always give, but you never ask."

IT'S ALL ABOUT RELATIONSHIPS

His words caught me off guard. Dan explained further.

"If you would just ask, people would bend over backwards to help you out—especially if you're asking the right tribe, the right people, the ones you've already helped or who know that you've helped others. It all comes full circle."

That advice hit home for not just me but Angie too. It was a reminder that reciprocity works both ways—not only do we need to give, but we also need to ask for help and allow ourselves to receive.

Of course, it's possible to ask for too much help too often. Perhaps you've encountered those who ask for help constantly but never give back in return. These folks inevitably become frustrated when people stop responding to their requests, not realizing that reciprocity requires a healthy balance of give and take.

Many people struggle with this balance. Some know they need help but are too proud or afraid to ask for it. Others may not even realize they need help until it's too late. And then there are the folks who expect help all the time.

Recently, we conducted a training session for a group that we've partnered with. I offered an hour and a half of my time teaching, answering questions, and helping people navigate their challenges. Notably, I didn't get paid for it; that wasn't the point. The goal was to simply contribute and offer value.

Five minutes after the session ended, we got a call from one of the participants asking for help with their business. I hadn't even mentioned that we could help them, much less try to sell our services, during the training. The relationship we'd built and the value I offered was enough to spark the opportunity.

So give generously without demanding anything in return, but don't be afraid to ask for help. That's our first and most important piece of advice when it comes to building relationships.

We embrace the idea of mutual growth. On our whiteboard, we have a simple reminder: "Be one percent better every day, and help everyone you come in contact with to be one percent better every day." This isn't just a mantra—it's a guiding principle for how we operate.

A great example of this comes from a recent client we brought on. When we first connected with him, he wasn't ready to commit, but we kept in touch. Over the next few months, we spoke three more times. Every time we interacted, he followed up with an email thanking us for our advice and sharing how he'd passed it on to his team. There was no pressure, no hard sell—just genuine relationship-building.

Eventually, out of the blue, he reached out and said, "Alright, I'm ready. Let's go."

Because we had built a solid foundation of trust, things moved quickly from that point on. We didn't need a week to get started—we needed just one day.

That's the power of asking, giving, and building trust. When you strike the right balance, opportunities will flow naturally, and the relationships you've nurtured along the way will pay dividends in ways you might never expect.

At the end of the day, business is not just about transactions—it's about relationships, connections, and being open to opportunities in whatever form they take. Sometimes, those opportunities come from the most unexpected places, and sometimes, simply showing up is enough to make all the difference.

IT'S ALL ABOUT RELATIONSHIPS

BRINGING YOUR WHOLE SELF TO THE TABLE

If you want to build genuine connections and create meaningful interactions—which is essential for any business—then you need to bring your whole self to the table. So many people bring only a part of themselves into a situation—they show up with a polished, pretend self, whether it's their sales persona or their professional mask.

But while that may feel safer, we've learned it's not what's best to do. We've discovered it's better to bring our authentic selves to every conversation. When we speak to a client or a candidate or a partner, we strive to have a real conversation, the same as we would with anyone else. Everyone we encounter meets the true versions of us.

Recently, for example, we had a conversation with a potential client, and while he was there physically, he wasn't really present. We could tell by his responses—*yep, sure, yeah*—that his mind was somewhere else. He was going through the motions, but he wasn't bringing his whole self to the conversation. And because of that, not only will he likely forget our discussion, but we walked away from the meeting not wanting to engage with him again. That lack of presence and authenticity creates a disconnect, and it can have a profound impact on whether or not a relationship moves forward.

So show up as your authentic, whole self, no matter who you're interacting with. Be present in the moment, fully engaged, and honest about who you are.

DOUBLING DOWN AS DUALPRENEURS

LOVING THE WORK MORE THAN THE JOB

Another point we'd like to emphasize is the importance of loving the work more than the job. We talk to so many people who aren't happy with their jobs. They don't like what they're doing, but they feel stuck because they need the paycheck.

On the other hand, we've all seen those rare examples of people who, despite having what others might consider a mundane job, are filled with joy. Think of the hard-working person digging a ditch or delivering packages who is smiling ear to ear.

The other day, we saw a group of landscapers working outside. One of them, the guy doing the weed whacking, was clearly enjoying himself. He wasn't just going through the motions—he was having fun with it. We watched him finish one spot and then literally skip over to the next, still smiling. Maybe he was just a naturally happy guy, or maybe he had found a way to truly enjoy his work. Either way, it was clear he was content with his daily life.

You see, it's not about the title or the position—it's about finding a way to love what you're doing and being great at it, no matter what it is.

BUILDING TRUST WITH INTEGRITY

Our next advice comes from something that we see often in the world of consulting. It certainly applies to leaders at all levels of an organization, but it applies more broadly to just about everyone. Here it is:

Before criticizing others, try to fix your own issues first!

IT'S ALL ABOUT RELATIONSHIPS

We get it. We're both coaches, so we have a natural tendency to see problems in other people or processes and want to fix them. However, not every situation calls for immediate correction.

For example, I (Travis) once made the mistake of calling out a CEO on a video call over what seemed like a minor issue. I have a habit of keeping way too many browser tabs open, and I noticed during the video call that this CEO had the same problem. Without thinking, I pointed it out in front of his team and offered to help him solve it. The CEO didn't take this well and bristled.

In hindsight, it's clear that I hadn't earned the right to criticize him in that setting, so the CEO was understandably upset. That moment reinforced for me the importance of tact, timing, and building enough trust before giving feedback.

Building trust means having integrity and always operating above board. This includes not lowering your standards just to close a deal. That rarely ends well.

Every now and then, a client will try to negotiate down our standard fee, and we've been tempted to say, "Sure, we can lower the fee just this once." However, we've learned that any time we negotiate on something we know we shouldn't, bad things happen. We essentially set ourselves up for future problems. When we've caved and agreed to a lower fee or an extension of our guarantee without the usual terms and restrictions, it almost always comes back to bite us.

That's why it's so important to draw clear boundaries and stand firm on what you know is right for your business. Compromising your standards not only dilutes your brand, but it also invites more complications down the line.

SURROUND YOURSELF WITH GREAT PEOPLE

One of the most valuable lessons we've learned is the importance of surrounding ourselves with great people. It's a lesson that's been repeated to us over the years in books and by mentors, but for a long time, we didn't fully grasp its significance.

You've probably heard the saying, "If you're the smartest person in the room, you're in the wrong room." We believe this is true, but we've also learned that it's not just about being around smart people—it's about being around the *right* people, the people who believe in us, who see our potential, and who want to push us forward rather than hold us back.

It's easy to overlook how the wrong people in your circle can hinder your progress. If you're surrounded by individuals who don't believe in your vision, who constantly question your goals or tell you that what you're trying to achieve isn't possible, it can drag you down. We've seen this happen time and time again, both in our own lives and in the lives of others.

In the early stages of our business, we didn't fully believe in our own potential. A big reason was that we had the wrong people in our tribe. We had people telling us we couldn't do it, that our goals were too ambitious, that what we were trying to accomplish simply wouldn't work. It's hard to dream big when the voices around you constantly pull you back down into small thinking.

Things changed when we started surrounding ourselves with a different type of person. Now, instead of hearing, "You can't do that," we hear, "Why aren't you doing more?" This shift was transformative. Instead of people casting doubt on our abilities, we're now surrounded by people who push us to go further, to dream bigger, and to take even bolder steps toward our goals.

IT'S ALL ABOUT RELATIONSHIPS

Today, we're fortunate to have people in our network who we never thought we'd be connected with—people who have achieved extraordinary things. We have multi-millionaires in our circle now, and while their wealth doesn't define them or our relationship with them, we've come to realize that their mindset does. Every time we talk to them, we learn something new. And one of the most interesting things they've shared is that they too are constantly learning from others who are further along the path than they are.

It doesn't matter whether you're a millionaire or just getting by—you need to be surrounded by people who are always pushing you to be better, who support your vision, who encourage your ambition, and who aren't trying to pull you back, whether intentionally or unintentionally.

The right tribe will lift you higher. They will see the potential in you that you might not even see in yourself yet, and they will challenge you to reach it. That's the power of surrounding yourself with great people, and it's a lesson we now hold close in everything we do.

Ultimately, success in business and life comes from being clear, being authentic, and loving what you do. Whether it's bringing your whole self to the table, staying fully present, surrounding yourself with the right people, or standing firm in your values, these principles create a foundation for strong relationships and sustainable success.

CHAPTER FIVE
REAL COMMUNICATION

THE FOUNDATION OF ANY SUCCESSFUL business partnership—or any partnership really—is the ability to communicate openly and effectively with each other. This may sound straightforward, but in reality, it's a delicate balance that requires constant attention. While honesty is important, so is delivery. Being brutally honest can be effective, but we've learned we must be tactful—*always*.

To that end, we work hard with all of our clients and partners to make sure we communicate with one another honestly and clearly. And that means we have to be OK when our communication misses the mark. It's inevitable that we'll sometimes misunderstand each other or that one of us will take something the wrong way. In those moments, we need to check our egos at the door and not let the small things build into larger issues.

Just remember, what might seem small to one person could be a huge deal to the other—and vice versa. We have to recognize that just because something feels insignificant to us doesn't mean it isn't meaningful to someone else. Understanding that difference is key. But no matter what, we have to keep the lines of communication open, even when it's uncomfortable or when we've taken a misstep.

Beyond communicating well with each other, it's equally important to understand the communication styles of the people we work with. Different people communicate in different ways. Some people are aggressive and direct while others are reserved and shy. Some people thrive on action and decision-making while others take a passive approach. The challenge is to adapt to these varying styles without abandoning the structure and process that ensures effective communication.

CRUCIAL CONVERSATIONS

The good news is that communication is a skill that can be learned and developed. We use a technique called Crucial Conversations, which are tactics from a book by the same name.[2] A Crucial Conversation is both a skill and an artform. It starts from the heart where you approach discussions with an open mind and recognize that your perspective is not the sole truth. The goal is to create a safe environment where honest communication can thrive and to avoid getting hooked by emotion.

While emotions are natural, letting them dictate the direction of a discussion is rarely productive. Try to stick to the facts and focus on what is true and actionable. This will help you turn what could be a chaotic, emotional exchange into a constructive dialogue that leads to real progress. The conversation should aim to establish a mutual goal and lead to agreement on a clear plan that both parties can commit to.

Too many people dive into conversations based solely on what's happening in the moment and what they feel, reacting rather than thinking strategically. Take, for example, a situation I (Angie) experienced with a previous boss. One day, my Slack notifications started blowing up. When Travis asked if I had a meeting scheduled, I replied, "No, it's just my boss."

As it turned out, this impromptu interaction was about putting out a perceived fire. My boss and I spent half an hour on the phone discussing everything that was going wrong. In reality, not only did it end up being a wasted half hour, but more time was lost as others had to scramble to fix problems that might not have been actual emergencies.

I finally scheduled a formal meeting with my boss and titled it "A Crucial Conversation." I pointed out that if this reactive behavior (turning every situation into a fire drill) was happening with me, it was likely happening with everyone else in the company. During our discussion, I made the environment safe for honest feedback and, after navigating some initial ego defenses, my boss slowly but surely began to change her approach.

My leader and I also ended up introducing the Thomas-Kilmann Conflict Mode Instrument (Figure 3)[3] as a way to make sure everyone was "fighting fair" and working toward a mutually beneficial agreement. It was especially helpful when certain team members or even entire teams were at odds.

The matrix identifies five different approaches to handling conflict, which are based on two dimensions: *assertiveness* (focusing on your own needs) and *cooperativeness* (focusing on the needs of others). Each of the five conflict styles—competing, collaborating, compromising, avoiding, and accommodating—come with their own strengths and drawbacks, depending on the situation and who you are talking to.

By using the matrix, you can choose the most effective conflict style based on the current situation and the desired outcome of both parties.

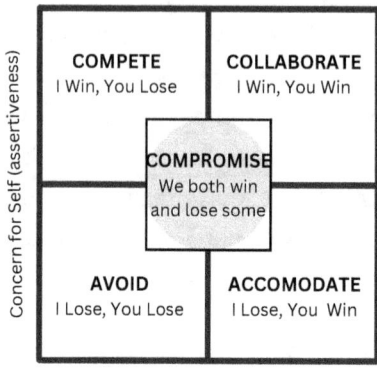

FIGURE 3

Communication requires a blend of process and emotional intelligence (EQ). You need a consistent structure to guide the conversation, but you also need enough awareness to adjust your approach based on who you're speaking with.

When Travis accidentally offended that CEO by mentioning his many browser tabs, he was merely trying to make a harmless, lighthearted comment. However, what was harmless and lighthearted to Travis was rude and offensive to the CEO. This difference in communication styles led to a misunderstanding. A comment that was meant to be good-natured crossed a boundary and caused an issue. Travis clearly had not earned the right to say it.

That's the thing about communication: You have to earn the right to say certain things, particularly when offering feedback or criticism. It's easy to assume that honesty is enough, but honesty without the right foundation can do more harm than good.

Ultimately, communication in business isn't just about talking. It's about understanding who you're speaking with, adapting your approach to their style, and ensuring you've earned the right to speak candidly. The balance of structure and EQ is essential to fostering strong, lasting partnerships.

SETTING CLEAR BOUNDARIES

Part of honest communication is setting clear boundaries. You need to define how your relationships—both professional and personal—should function. When I (Travis) first started recruiting, I treated it like one of my old jobs. If a boss called me at nine o'clock at night, I'd feel obligated to answer the phone. I never set proper boundaries with my boss, and that carried over to my interactions with clients. I would answer their late-night calls without question, and once I started doing that, it set a precedent and became an expectation.

Nowadays, both Angie and I take a different approach. When we bring on a new client, we make it crystal clear from the beginning how we work and how our relationship will operate. We draw the lines, and we let everyone know what to expect. It's much easier to communicate those boundaries upfront than to try to correct course later on when things have already spiraled out of control.

But it's not just about setting boundaries for our personal time—it's also about understanding the role we play in someone's development. Being a coach is very different from being a sponsor. Sometimes, we're just there to support someone, to offer a bit of encouragement, and help them along the way. Other times, our job is to help them improve, even if that means pushing them outside of their comfort zone.

Recently, we had a candidate who absolutely bombed his first screening interview. We weren't planning to send him on to the client, but he asked for feedback and coaching. We gave it to him, and a month later, he reached out again. He had made changes and worked on himself, and he had another interview lined up. Unfortunately, he bombed it too. Disappointed, he called me afterward and said, "I could really use some help."

So I gave him some coaching, and he'll probably do better in his next interview. But then he asked if he could call us every time he needed help. I had to be honest with him and say, "No, I can't be there every time. I can offer a little help along the way, but there are many other resources out there to help you improve as well."

The reality is that we speak to thousands of candidates—we simply can't be there for each one every time they stumble. And this boundary has to be set and clearly communicated early in the relationship.

It's also important to have a goal in mind when communicating with someone. Communication is never a one-size-fits-all endeavor. Sometimes it bobs and weaves in unexpected directions. We experience this all the time. We may start off trying to communicate in one way, and it ends up going in another direction entirely. Having a goal for the exchange helps us get back to what the conversation needs to accomplish.

Try to remain adaptable while staying grounded in clear, thoughtful communication. Again, it's a skill that you can develop, and when done well, it can make all the difference in maintaining strong, successful relationships.

REAL COMMUNICATION

GETTING BETTER AT COMMUNICATING

We keep saying that communication is a skill, but what if you're just not good at it? If you're someone who struggles with communication, and it doesn't come naturally to you, there are ways to develop the skill.

One of the simplest and most effective ways is to ask questions. When we're on a call with someone who is introverted or uncomfortable with the conversation, we don't dive straight into business. Instead, we ask a lot of questions. We try to understand where they're coming from and what's going on in their world. We aim to recognize when we need to warm up with small talk, like chatting about the weather.

Learning to understand different personality types can also be a huge help. It's usually not hard to figure out who falls on which end of the communication spectrum. If we're speaking with someone assertive or aggressive, we know we need to approach the conversation differently than we would with someone who is withdrawn and quiet.

Pay attention and observe people, and you'll start to get better at communicating with them. Think of it like playing poker. The best poker players spend hours watching their opponents, studying their behavior, and picking up on "tells." Effective communication is much the same. You need to read the room and try to understand the cues people are giving you.

For example, if someone is sitting there looking frustrated or upset, you should know right away that either you did something to bother them, or something happened to them before the conversation even started. In that case, it might not be the best time to dive into a deep discussion.

DOUBLING DOWN AS DUALPRENEURS

Ultimately, communication is about understanding the other person's needs and adapting your approach accordingly—whether by asking the right questions, studying body language, or simply being present in the moment. In fact, being present is one of the most important elements of being a good communicator. Remember these nine rules:

Nine Rules for Being Present

1 Don't multitask. Turn off your cell phone and eliminate distractions.
2 Don't pontificate. Keep your personal opinions to yourself.
3 Ask open-ended questions.
4 Go with the flow. Thoughts will come in as the other person talks, so write them down. That way you can come back to them after the other person has finished talking.
5 If you don't know the answer, it's OK to share that, but promise to get back to them with the answer.
6 Don't equate your experience to theirs. The discussions you have with employees and clients are about their experience, not yours.
7 Don't repeat yourself. Stay crisp, focused, and on point.
8 Listen. If your mouth is open, you're not learning more about their needs.
9 Be brief. Be bright. Be gone. Be interested in the people you are talking with and respect their time.

Far too often, conflicts arise because people fail to do these basic things. Take, for example, two business partners struggling to see eye to eye. Imagine them on a call in the midst of ongoing conflict. They might even be going through co-founder therapy, which is becoming more common in the business world.

REAL COMMUNICATION

One partner is the technical expert, deeply immersed in the product or service. The other is the sales driver, focused on growing the business. But they don't understand each other's roles, let alone how the other person operates. One believes they should be working ninety hours a week, while the other thinks fifty hours is plenty and insists on taking lunch breaks.

Without paying attention to each other's perspectives, they might jump on a call and immediately start arguing, going at it without taking a step back to think about what's really going on or how they can work through their differences. They're both stuck in their own mindset, unable to appreciate where the other is coming from.

We recently gave advice to a friend who found himself in a similar situation. He and his co-founder were at odds, and their conflict came to a head during an important sales trip. The other co-founder invited our friend to fly to New York with him for a client meeting—something our friend hadn't even known was on the agenda. As they were heading to the airport, the co-founder casually mentioned that they had another meeting that day with a potential new client, a big client. It was a big opportunity, but our friend had no presentation planned, no deck prepared—nothing. Despite the lack of preparation, they went in, and our friend did his best.

He admitted afterward that it wasn't his best presentation, and while they didn't close the deal, he managed to create a champion within the company. That champion booked their next meeting, which is a significant achievement in enterprise sales where decisions are rarely made on the spot.

Instead of celebrating this victory, when they got into the car, the co-founder started berating our friend for blowing the deal. He didn't understand how enterprise sales work. He expected immediate results and didn't recognize the value in securing a follow-up meeting.

Our suggestion to our friend was simple: For their next meeting, build out a strong presentation deck, put together a solid plan, and then ask the co-founder for feedback before presenting. Say, "I know I didn't do as well last time, so can I run this by you beforehand and get your thoughts?" By doing this, they'd be able to communicate better, align their expectations, and hopefully find common ground.

It may seem like a rough process, but by bringing the co-founder into the preparation stage, they could start communicating more effectively and ensure that when the presentation happened, both would be on the same page. The presentation would now reflect something they both believed in, and that's key to moving forward as partners.

The lesson here is clear: By paying attention, asking questions, and being open to feedback, conflicts that seem insurmountable can be resolved. Communication isn't just about talking; it's about truly listening, understanding, and adapting to the needs and perspectives of others. In business, as in life, that makes all the difference.

COACHING BASED ON DATA

Now, we've said you need to avoid getting hooked on emotion. Feelings are natural, yes, but when feelings guide a conversation, it can quickly go off the rails. Therefore, regardless of the situation, whether it's a formal coaching session or a casual conversation, our philosophy remains the same: We coach based on data, not gut feelings.

We've seen far too many people fall into the trap of making decisions and offering guidance driven by fear, concern, or instinct rather than solid evidence. A prime example of this occurred during my (Travis) time at Fivestars. They were on a roll, achieving record-breaking results month after month, until Facebook changed its algorithms. Suddenly, things took a downturn, and the leadership started giving direction and coaching based on their gut reactions rather than the data that had previously guided the company's success.

These days, when we coach as part of our recruitment process or even when we take on a new client project, key performance indicators (KPIs) become our rock-solid foundation. For example, if a salesperson is performing exceptionally well, we examine every data point to understand what they're doing right, and if they're struggling, we take the same data-driven approach.

Let's say a salesperson typically closes twenty deals a month, with sixty presentations required to achieve it, and to reach those sixty presentations, they need to make eighty dials a day with two hours of talk time. We don't micromanage the numbers, but when certain actions historically lead to success, we use that data to guide our coaching. In other words, we don't push for a specific number of dials or talk time unless that's what the data shows is necessary for success.

However, if a salesperson who consistently hits 130 percent of their plan suddenly drops to eighty percent, and the data reflects that change, it's a good starting point for a conversation. When we approach the discussion with data in hand, we usually find that the individual is more likely to engage constructively. Instead of arguing over subjective impressions, they can look at the numbers and identify what went wrong themselves.

Once we've identified the issue, we might dig a little deeper by reviewing their calls. Maybe we'll discover that they started omitting key elements in their pitch that they previously included. Whether in sales or any other area, coaching based on data matters because data doesn't lie; it simply reflects the reality of the situation.

When someone fails to meet a deadline, it's not enough for them to simply say, "I didn't hit that deadline last week because of X, Y, and Z." The real question is, what does the data say? If we look at the data from the previous months and see that they consistently hit their targets, but in the last two weeks they haven't, we need to ask, "Why do you think that is?" Often, this leads to a realization: They're not doing what they're supposed to do.

We recently faced a challenging situation involving a partner who referred his best friend as a candidate that we submitted to a client. The candidate had an interview, but afterward, he failed to follow up promptly and waited eight hours before reaching out. In a sales role and even a project consulting conversation, immediate follow-up is critical. A delay suggests to the client that the candidate might not perform promptly in the job itself. As a result, in this case, the candidate didn't advance to the next round.

Our partner was understandably upset and sent an emotionally charged email to us and to all the other recruiters. In the email, he criticized the client and questioned our process. I (Angie) was initially quite upset, but I decided not to respond immediately. I recognized that the email was driven by emotion rather than facts.

We chose to take a step back, consider the situation carefully, and focus on the data and the facts before replying. Although some of the partner's points were valid, much of the frustration was misplaced.

In a high-stress situation, when patience wears thin and emotions run high, communication becomes far more difficult, so it's more important than ever to make sure you're acting on the data and facts.

REACHING OUT REGULARLY

Of course, if you want to have the hard facts about what's going on throughout your organization, then you need to have regular, consistent, intentional engagement with your team members. Regular and structured interactions, like one-on-ones and coaching calls, are essential for growth and success. But it's not just about frequency; it's about quality. Being present, prepared, and following through on commitments are necessary components of effective leadership.

Unfortunately, this level of engagement rarely takes place in some businesses. We've experienced firsthand how damaging it can be when managers fail to prioritize these interactions. I (Travis) once had a manager who almost always canceled her one-on-ones at the last minute. When she did have them, she wasn't prepared, wasn't engaged, and often didn't follow through on action items. This left me feeling that these meetings were a complete waste of time.

If we were to ask fifteen leaders right now, whether they're in sales, project management, or any other field, "How many times per week do you have intentional, planned interactions with each member of your team?"—the answers would reveal much about their leadership effectiveness. Regular, purposeful "touches," or one-on-one conversations, are absolutely necessary because they build trust, ensure alignment, and keep everyone focused on their goals. They also make sure you know exactly what is going on in your organization so you can deal with the reality and not just gut feelings and suspicions.

In fact, we'd go so far as to say effective leadership is only possible when you maintain regular, intentional interactions with your team members. The structure and frequency of these touches can make all the difference in whether your team feels supported, engaged, and aligned with their goals.

You have to establish a cadence for these touches—a rhythm that ensures you are regularly checking in, providing feedback, and staying connected with your team. For our one-on-one meetings, we use the framework in Figure 4 because it provides a consistent structure that ensures each meeting is productive and mutually beneficial.

1:1 Meeting Framework

30-Minute 1:1 Timebox
- 10 minutes - them
- 10 minutes - you
- 10 minutes - development/career/growth

60-Minute 1:1 Timebox
- 15 minutes - them
- 15 minutes - #'s/KPIs, pacing, etc.
- 15 minutes - pipeline discussion
- 15 minutes - development/career/growth

Discussion topics
1. Short-term / long-term goals
2. Roadblocks
3. Relationships
4. When are you most/least productive?
5. How are the projects going?
6. What can I do to make your work easier?
7. Where can I improve?

Questions to Ask
1. Tell me about what you've been working on.
2. Tell me about your week - what's it been like?
3. Tell me about your family / weekend / activities.
4. Tell me about any challenges you are having.
5. Would you update me on the X project?
6. What questions do you have about X?
7. How can I assist you? Where can I be helpful? What can I take off your plate?
8. What are your thoughts on X changes?
9. What can you / we do differently or better next time?

FIGURE 4

REAL COMMUNICATION

DATA-DRIVEN COMMUNICATION

So let's boil it all down. Here is the playbook we've used to ensure effective communication with partners, clients, and team members.

1. **Lead by coaching, training, motivating, and developing.** Remember, great leadership begins with a commitment to continuous coaching. It's not a one-time event or a one-size-fits-all approach. It's an ongoing process of guiding, teaching, and motivating your team to reach their full potential. As a leader, your role is to be a coach, not just a manager. Your success is measured by your ability to develop others into successful, self-sufficient professionals.

2. **Establish a team mission/vision.** A team without a clear mission or vision is like a ship without a rudder. It's your job to establish and communicate a strong mission and vision that everyone on the team can rally around. This vision should be more than just hitting goals and targets; it should encompass the values, goals, and culture you want to build within your team. This shared purpose will keep the team focused and aligned, especially during challenging times.

3. **Be present with your team and help them win (player-coach).** The most effective leaders are in the trenches with their team. A player-coach is visible, accessible, and actively involved in the day-to-day activities of their team.

4. **Remove any and all obstacles (servant leadership).** As a leader, one of your primary responsibilities is to remove obstacles that may hinder your team's performance. This is where servant

leadership comes into play. By focusing on the needs of your team and working tirelessly to eliminate any barriers to their success, you create an environment where they can thrive.

5. **Be a subject matter expert (SME).** You can't coach what you don't know. To lead a winning team, you must be a subject matter expert in your field. This means staying up-to-date with industry trends, understanding the products or services you're selling, and mastering your processes. Your expertise not only builds your credibility but also allows you to provide valuable insights and guidance to your team.

6. **Get to know your team.** Take the time to learn about their personal interests, values, and career aspirations. This knowledge will help you tailor your coaching to their individual needs and motivations. Additionally, look for valuable qualities such as an entrepreneurial mindset, drive, coachability, passion for success, integrity, energy, and enthusiasm. These are the traits that often distinguish high performers, and your job is to nurture and develop these qualities across the team.

7. **Practice continuous process improvement.** It's your responsibility to understand current processes and make quick improvements where necessary. Be curious, ask questions, and seek to understand why things are done a certain way. Identify what's working and build on previous successes. At the same time, look for areas that need improvement. Sometimes, it's not about replacing the wheel but simply tightening the spokes to ensure everything runs smoothly.

8. **Establish a daily cadence.** A strategic and successful process only works when it is consistently followed. Establish a daily

cadence that everyone believes in and adheres to. This includes knowing all KPIs and coaching your team on them. Every team member needs a clear path to success, and it's your job to provide that.

9 **Embody winning leadership characteristics.** To lead a winning team, you must embody the following characteristics: inspiration, motivation, integrity, energy, flexibility, metrics-driven focus, and a sense of fun. These traits not only define your leadership style but also set the tone for your team's culture. Remember this mantra: "Have fun, keep score, and win!" It's a simple yet powerful philosophy that keeps the team motivated and focused on the right objectives.

Additionally, we recommend the following daily routines. These routines were developed particularly for sales leaders (as you'll see), but they can be adapted for just about any role or industry.

Daily Routines for Success

Start each day with a **morning stand-up** where the team can discuss wins and challenges from the previous day. This is also an opportunity for mental preparation, whether through role-playing, discussing a new article, or sharing other valuable insights.

Throughout the day, make it a point to be **side by side** with your team. Plan the top priorities with each rep early every morning and observe their calls, offering coaching as needed. Join calls when necessary, leveraging your expertise to close deals and demonstrate best practices.

Weekly **one-on-one meetings** with each team member are absolutely essential. Dedicate an hour for each session, divided into four fifteen-minute segments: rep time, numbers/KPIs, pipeline review, and development. Additionally, engage in **call coaching** with each rep at least twice a week. Have them send you three calls per week—two for coaching and one "rockstar" call to share with the team.

End the week with a **team meeting** where you provide updates, review numbers, conduct training, and celebrate rockstar calls. This not only reinforces the team's progress but also fosters a sense of camaraderie and shared purpose.

Ultimately, effective leaders are good communicators who are able to coach, motivate, and develop their team. They create safe environments where people can discuss issues openly and honestly, they focus on what the data says, adapt their communication style based on who they're talking to, and maintain regular and consistent contact with partners, team members, clients, and candidates. You don't need to already possess an innate talent for communication. You can hone your ability, learn from missteps, and get better at it, just as you can work on any skill and get better over time.

PART THREE
TACTICAL TOOLS

CHAPTER SIX

DUMB THINGS TO AVOID

THE MOST IMPORTANT LESSONS ARE often learned from the mistakes we make, and we have definitely made some mistakes.

When we started our first business, GSD Coach & Recruiting, we jumped in headfirst without doing any real advanced planning. As a result, we made some unfortunate decisions, and later on, we had to take a step back and correct a few things.

Spare yourself the hassle by taking the time to lay the right foundation from the outset. Selecting a general set of services, creating a name, and designing a logo only scratch the surface of what's required to start a business. These initial steps may be exciting and visually rewarding, but they don't even begin to address the more complex aspects that determine whether or not your business will succeed in the long run. Before diving into the fun parts, there are some important things that need to be addressed to ensure your business has a solid foundation.

DON'T RUSH INTO YOUR LEGAL AND TAX DESIGNATIONS

One of the first and most important steps before launching any business is to get professional legal and tax advice. We learned this the hard way because we didn't fully understand all of the legal and tax ramifications of our business model, and it caused a bunch of headaches down the road.

The business structure you choose—whether it's a sole proprietorship, LLC, partnership, or corporation—has significant implications for how you'll pay taxes, the amount of personal liability you'll assume, and how you'll manage the administrative side of your business. Each structure has different requirements for federal, state, and local taxes, including tax withholding and the deductibility of expenses.

When we first started GSD, we opted for a sole proprietorship. At that stage, it was straightforward, allowing us to pay taxes once a year. However, as the business grew and became profitable, this structure became less efficient.

About three years in, we transitioned to an S-Corp. This move simplified our tax filings and made it easier to submit realistic quarterly tax payments. The S-Corp structure also provided more flexibility in how we could manage and distribute income, which saved us money and reduced stress during tax season.

DON'T TRY TO BE EVERYTHING TO EVERYONE

Once the legal and tax frameworks are squared away, the real fun begins. Now it's time to define the specific consulting or service area your business will focus on. This is where your unique expertise comes into play. For us, it was clear that we had a strong background in sales, recruiting, coaching, process improvement, and project management. However, simply knowing your areas of expertise isn't enough. You need to clearly define the niche you want to serve and tailor your offerings accordingly.

Initially, we made the classic mistake of trying to be everything to everyone. We believed we could serve all types of clients, big and small, and we tried to do everything—consulting work, fractional sales and project management roles, reference checks, and more. But trying to be everything to everyone doesn't lead to success. For us, it quickly proved to be a waste of time, energy, and resources. It left us feeling burnt out and, more importantly, cost us money. We soon realized that to be successful, we needed to narrow our focus and become specialists rather than generalists.

After some reflection and analysis, we pivoted to concentrate on recruiting within the SaaS domain as well as project management consulting and training for small businesses, specifically targeting startup clients with small sales or project management teams, or those still engaged in founder-led sales or with an ineffective PMO. We still do some related tasks, like reference checks, but we no longer offer services like coaching, background checks, or drug testing. These non-core services are now handled by other providers.

This focused approach allowed us to understand the specific needs of these startup companies and become experts in hiring for their sales teams and marketing and customer success roles as well as serving as project management consultants and trainers. By specializing, we were able to provide higher value to our clients, which in turn increased our profitability and reputation in the industry.

DON'T SET YOUR TARGET CLIENTS TOO BROADLY

Once you've defined your service area, the next logical step is to identify the types of clients you want to serve. For us, this meant considering several factors such as the size of the company, its level of maturity, and who our main point of contact would be. It's easy to assume you can serve anyone and everyone, but in reality, trying to do so will stretch your resources thin and dilute your effectiveness.

We initially believed we could handle clients of all sizes and levels of maturity, but this approach didn't work. So instead, we honed in on a more specific client profile: small businesses and startup companies in the SaaS sector that were either building small sales or project management teams, or still involved in founder-led sales or with an ineffective PMO. This decision allowed us to streamline our operations and focus on delivering exceptional value to a specific type of client rather than trying to be a jack-of-all-trades.

DON'T OVERLOOK A REMOTE SERVICE DELIVERY MODEL

One of the best lessons we learned early on was the efficiency of a remote service delivery model. We discovered that we could be just as effective—if not more so—working from our home offices than we would be if we were traveling to client locations. This was particularly true given that many of our clients were based in different U.S. states, in Canada, and internationally. In most cases, in-person meetings were impractical or unnecessary.

Our remote model not only saved us time and money but also allowed us to scale our business more efficiently. We could take on more clients without the constraints of travel, and we were able to offer competitive pricing because of our lower overhead costs. This model also helped us attract clients who valued flexibility and efficiency, which further solidified our niche in the market.

DON'T SELECT THE WRONG REVENUE MODEL

With our services defined and our target clients identified, the next step was to develop a sustainable revenue model. We evaluated different pricing structures based on the nature of the projects and clients we were taking on. For most recruiting projects, we settled on a one-time fee—a percentage of the candidate's annual base salary—that covered the entire project. This approach incentivized us to be efficient; the quicker we completed the project, the more profitable it became. For the project management consulting and training projects, we found that a statement of work charging by the hour for a given deliverable within a given timeframe was most effective, especially for small businesses.

However, we recognized the need to mitigate risk, particularly with clients who might be slower to make decisions or prone to changing job or project requirements. For these higher-risk clients, we decided to charge a retainer. This would ensure that we received some revenue upfront, even if the project took longer than expected or the client made changes that required additional work.

This hybrid approach allowed us to balance profitability with risk management, which ensured that our business would remain financially stable even when faced with challenging projects.

DOUBLING DOWN AS DUALPRENEURS

Just remember, when you start a business, it's easy to fall into the trap of spending a lot of time and money with little to show for it. This often comes down to one critical oversight: pricing. You need to get your pricing structure right from the start. Too many entrepreneurs overlook pricing in the rush to land their first deal.

Just the other day, we spoke with someone who had been in recruiting for fifteen years but had only recently opened their own business. When we asked about their pricing, the response was troubling: "Whatever I can do to close a deal right now."

This mindset is a huge red flag. Going too low on pricing might close a deal, but it also risks sending the wrong message. When you undervalue your services, potential clients will start to question your competence.

We know because we made this exact mistake. When we started GSD, we significantly undervalued our services. As a result, we were barely profitable. The turning point came when a prospective client said they wouldn't work with us because our prices were too low. They equated our lower pricing with lower quality, and that was the moment we realized we needed to charge what we were worth.

Pricing isn't about what the market can bear but what the market expects from a top-tier service provider. Think about the value you are delivering to clients and the breadth and depth of experience you bring to the table and price yourself accordingly. Undervaluing your services does more than hurt your bottom line—it undermines your credibility.

One thing we've noticed is that the clients who push the hardest for lower prices often become the most difficult to work with. They tend to negotiate the hardest and demand the most, which rarely justifies the lower fee. So be sure to value yourself and your services properly, and you'll attract clients who value you too.

As we adjusted our pricing, we also took a step back to set some serious goals. We established some Big Hairy Audacious Goals

(BHAGs)[4] alongside realistic targets and absolute minimums. Every month now, we review our progress and recalibrate as needed.

The key lesson here is to understand your worth, set audacious goals, and build processes that support your journey. Pricing yourself too low not only diminishes your value in the eyes of potential clients but can also stall your business before it truly gets off the ground.

DON'T CONFUSE MANAGING THE WORK WITH DOING THE WORK

Next, we had to figure out how to manage the actual delivery of our services. We split this into two distinct workstreams: managing the work and doing the work. I (Travis) took the lead on doing the work, which chiefly involved sourcing candidates for our clients. This was the core of our business, and my expertise in this area was central to our success.

On the other hand, I (Angie) focused on managing the work. This encompassed all the back-office operations and all project management activities, such as developing and sending candidate profiles, handling invoicing, and managing relationships with our partners. By dividing these responsibilities, we were able to play to our strengths and ensure that both the front-end and back-end of the business were running smoothly. Failing to make this distinction between managing the work and doing the work can make your processes less efficient and lead to tension in the team as you inadvertently step on each other's toes.

DON'T TRY TO WING IT (CREATE SCRIPTS!)

We are firm believers in the power of scripting. Without a clear script, your sales and project consulting conversations may lead to miscommunication and missed opportunities. Your team may struggle to address objections effectively or articulate the value of your product or service.

Therefore, even before we fully knew what we were doing, we made sure we had our scripts ready. These scripts weren't just about closing deals; they were about having meaningful conversations that allowed us to truly understand what our clients needed. Too often, new entrepreneurs jump into calls and immediately push for the close, but our approach was the opposite.

Our script focused on qualifying the client first, so we would start by letting them tell us about their pain points and what they were looking to achieve. Only if it made sense would we dive deeper and ask more probing questions to uncover the core of their needs. At that point, we would explain how our services could help them, which eventually led to a discussion about pricing.

This approach helped us make sure we were only moving forward with clients whose needs genuinely aligned with what we had to offer. And we do the same thing with our other project management consulting business.

Scripting also helps us say no when we need to. Just this week, we walked away from a potential client because they wanted to push beyond the boundaries of our contract and the way we work. Initially, we had different opinions on the matter, but ultimately, we agreed that sticking to our terms was the right choice. So we said no—and guess what? They reconsidered and came back to us on our terms. The ability to walk away from a deal when it's not the right fit is invaluable.

DUMB THINGS TO AVOID

DON'T FAIL TO EVALUATE POTENTIAL CLIENTS

Another important strategy we implemented was creating a matrix to evaluate potential clients as green, yellow, or red flag clients. Unless you evaluate potential clients, it's easy to fall into the trap of accepting any client that comes along. However, not every client is worth our time. Clients who meet all the green criteria are a go. If they fall into the yellow category, we take the time to dig deeper and have a more detailed conversation. If they're red, we walk away.

A good policy to adopt, one that has served us well, is this: If you wouldn't feel comfortable with your children working at that company, you probably shouldn't be recruiting or working on projects for them. This guiding principle has helped us maintain a high standard of integrity in our client relationships and ensured that we only partner with organizations we truly believe in.

AVOID A SHOTGUN APPROACH

Another hard lesson we learned early on was the ineffectiveness of a "shotgun approach"—throwing ourselves into everything, assuming that sheer activity will lead to success. We would get up in the morning and dive straight into work because we thought staying busy meant being productive. But we quickly realized that activity does not equal accomplishment.

This scattered approach in which we focused on completing small tasks like checking emails or responding to minor requests ended up being a huge distraction. It didn't move the needle on the important goals we needed to achieve.

Eventually, we learned to take a step back and prioritize. We implemented daily standups to understand what tasks were most critical, identify where blockers existed, and figure out how to resolve them. This structured approach was far more effective than just diving into a day filled to the brim with random tasks.

We also made the mistake of assuming that the more people we talked to, the better off we'd be. Our schedule was packed from morning to night with no breaks for eating, mental health, or anything else. We were constantly on the move, but we soon realized that this was not sustainable.

To fix the situation, we began blocking out time for breaks and not scheduling meetings back-to-back. We also started batching similar tasks together. Instead of having five different types of conversations back-to-back, we grouped similar discussions so we could maintain focus and efficiency. This simple change allowed us to have more meaningful conversations and reduced the mental exhaustion that comes from constantly switching gears.

By narrowing our focus and avoiding the shotgun approach, we were able to become much more effective and efficient in delivering our core services. This shift not only improved our productivity but also strengthened our reputation in the industry.

DON'T SELL YOURSELF SHORT

A final word of advice when you're laying the foundation for your new business: Don't sell yourself short. This goes back to what we said about pricing. It's amazing how often someone in a leadership role or a business owner doubts their own worth. Sometimes this is due to past feedback, when they were told their prices are too high or their product wasn't good enough, but this kind of self-doubt can easily become a significant barrier to success. You need to believe in the value of your services and stand behind your pricing.

In our own journey, we've encountered many instances where potential clients were surprised at how much value we offered for the price we charged. Years ago, that would have made us anxious. We would have been afraid that our prices were too high or that we needed to justify every cent. But over time, we've learned that the opposite is true. When you stand firm in the value you provide, you not only command respect but also attract clients who appreciate your work.

For many new business owners, this is a constant mental battle. The urge to take on any business at any price, just to have some revenue, is strong. But this mindset will undermine your business in the long run.

To overcome this hurdle, make sure to follow our steps in this chapter and put a solid business plan in place. Know what your services are, what your prices should be, and what your goals are. Revisit your plan regularly—every month or two—to see if anything needs tweaking. This "try, test, adjust" approach allows you to stay flexible while remaining confident in your value.

It's also important to take care of yourself mentally and physically. Starting a business requires grit, and that means staying healthy and maintaining a positive mindset.

Also, we strongly recommend getting a mentor. Find someone who has already done what you're trying to do, even if they're not in the same industry. It's OK to ask for help—pride shouldn't stand in the way of your success. People are often more willing to help than you might expect, especially if you ask the right people.

And be willing to become a mentor yourself. Even in the early stages, as you start figuring things out, there are always people who are a few steps behind you. Helping others will reinforce your own learning and build a supportive network around you.

In the beginning, we thought we knew everything, but clearly, we didn't. Reaching out to former bosses and successful people in similar fields for advice felt incredibly supportive, and it reassured us that we were on the right track.

HELPFUL TOOLS

A Checklist for Staying Grounded

- Don't let your ego get too big.
- Evaluate your job duties to determine if they can be done more efficiently.
- Learn to love change.
- Have fun!
- Don't sell yourself short.
- Get a mentor.
- Be a mentor.

DUMB THINGS TO AVOID

Business Plan Template

XX Business Plan
MM/DD/YYYY

Job(s) to Be Done from a Consumer's Perspective - xxx

Unique Business Idea - xxx

Target market - xxx

Business Plan

- Vision statement - xx
- Mission statement - xx
- Business description - xx
- Expertise - xx
- Qualifications - xx
- Industry Knowledge - xx

Service Offering/"Catalog"

Product/Service Offering	Scope	Duration	Fee

Analysis of the current market and opportunity

Region/City1	Region/City2	Region/City3	Region/City4

Five Year Forecast / Financial Plan

	2021	2022	2023	2024	2025
Revenue					
Expenses					

Launch Timing & Milestones - xxx

Fee Structure/Formula

- Cash compensation (salary + bonus) x 3. Take the above amount and divide by 261 working days in a year. Then divide that by 8 (hours in a day). That gives you your hourly rate. Assumptions: You multiple by 3 b/c that covers vacation plus the time you are doing admin work and not client work

CHAPTER SEVEN

DON'T CHASE SHINY OBJECTS

THE ALLURE OF NEW OPPORTUNITIES can be intoxicating, especially when you're an entrepreneur of a small business. Every day brings fresh ideas, potential partnerships, and innovative strategies that promise to take your business to the next level. It's very easy to get caught up in all the excitement, especially when those opportunities are presented by influential people. However, chasing after every new idea or opportunity without careful consideration can lead to a scattered focus and, ultimately, dilute your efforts.

Distinguishing between what's truly beneficial for your business and what is merely a distraction wrapped in the guise of opportunity is one the biggest challenges we all face as business owners. It requires a disciplined approach to decision-making. You have to understand that not every opportunity is worth pursuing, and even an idea that sounds good may pull you away from your goals and core objectives.

Being disciplined means saying no to distractions, no matter how tempting they might be, and maintaining a laser focus on your business's long-term goals. It's about making sure that every action you take is a step towards those goals. This is what separates effective leaders from those who are merely busy and caught up in a whirlwind of activities that ultimately don't move the needle.

You need to focus on doing the work that will genuinely advance your business, and that means prioritizing tasks and opportunities that align with your strategic objectives while ignoring the noise that threatens to derail your progress. We're not suggesting that you must be rigid or resistant to change—just selective and intentional about where you invest your time and resources.

By focusing on what truly matters, you can drive meaningful progress, build a stronger, more resilient business, and ensure that your efforts are always aligned with your vision. Remember, busyness is not a badge of honor. Productivity is. And productivity, in its truest sense, is about making smart decisions that propel your business forward, not just keeping yourself occupied.

ALIGNING ROLES AND RESPONSIBILITIES WITH STRENGTHS

In any business, but especially in a partnership, understanding and leveraging individual strengths is not just a nice-to-have—it's necessary for success. The roles and responsibilities that each partner takes on can make or break the business. When these are aligned with each person's strengths and passions, the result is not only greater efficiency but also a more fulfilling work environment.

When we started GSD, we soon realized that both of us trying to do everything was a recipe for burnout and mediocrity. We discovered that each of us has distinct strengths that, when properly aligned, will drive the business forward with far greater momentum than if we both try to wear every hat.

We started by acknowledging these strengths. Then, we made them the foundation of our respective roles within the business. To do that, we conducted a thorough audit of the work each of us was doing. We looked at every task, every responsibility, and then we asked ourselves a few key questions:

- Is this something I'm good at?
- Is this something I enjoy doing?
- Does this task play to my strengths?
- Does it energize me, or does it drain me?

This exercise wasn't just about splitting the workload—it was about ensuring that we were each working in our zone of genius as much as possible. The tasks that we each kept were those that aligned with our strengths and brought us joy.

When it came to the tasks that neither of us excelled at nor enjoyed, we had to make some tough decisions. Could we delegate or outsource these tasks to someone else? Could we automate them? Or were they simply unnecessary and should be stopped altogether?

John Wooden, the legendary basketball coach, once said, "Success is peace of mind, which is a direct result of self-satisfaction in knowing you did your best to become the best you are capable of becoming."[5] In other words, the quality of effort counts over 'winning.'"

This philosophy resonates with us deeply. Success in business isn't just about hitting financial targets or growing your client base; it's about making the best possible effort in everything you do. And the only way to make that kind of effort is to ensure that you're working from a place of strength and passion.

Beyond the practical benefits of aligning roles in your business with individual strengths, there's an emotional component that's just as important. When you're working in a role that suits your strengths, you're more likely to feel fulfilled, energized, and motivated. This isn't just good for productivity, it's good for your overall well-being.

On the other hand, when you're stuck doing work that doesn't align with your strengths, it can be draining and demoralizing. Over time, this can lead to burnout, resentment, and a lack of engagement. By clearly defining your role and focusing on what you do best, you can avoid these pitfalls and create a work environment that is not only productive but also enjoyable.

And when it comes to tasks that you neither excel at nor enjoy, be sure to eliminate or delegate them. But keep in mind that delegation isn't just about handing off tasks you don't want to do. Rather, it's about recognizing that someone else might be better suited for those tasks. You are placing your trust in someone and letting go of the need to control every aspect of the business.

Elimination is the other side of the coin. Not every task is necessary. Some activities may have once served a purpose but are now just taking up space in your schedule. By regularly auditing your responsibilities, tasks, and schedule, you can eliminate the dead weight that slows you down.

We approach delegation and elimination systematically. First, we identify the tasks that neither of us want to do nor are particularly good at. Then, we consider whether those tasks are essential to the business. If they are, we look for ways to delegate them, either to a team member or to an external service. If they aren't essential, we eliminate them altogether. This process is liberating because it allows us to focus on the work that truly matters and that we are passionate about.

Of course, our roles and responsibilities aren't set in stone. As the business evolves, so too must our roles. What worked a year ago might not work today, and what energizes us now might not be as fulfilling in the future. That's why it's important to regularly revisit and reassess our roles and responsibilities. This kind of flexibility allows us to adapt to changes in the business and in our personal lives, and it ensures that we're always working in alignment with our strengths and passions.

That doesn't mean we change roles on a whim. Instead, we approach changes thoughtfully, always considering the impact it may have on the business and on each other. And when changes are necessary, we make them in a way that supports our long-term goals and preserves the balance that keeps our partnership strong.

We've learned the key to success isn't just hard work—it's doing the *right* work at the *right* time, the work that we're best at and that we love. By conducting regular audits, delegating and eliminating tasks that don't align with our skills, and remaining flexible in our roles, we've been able to build two businesses that play to our individual and collective strengths. This approach has not only made us more effective as business partners but has also strengthened our partnership and enriched our lives.

In the end, a business is only as strong as the people behind it. When those people are working from a place of strength and passion, the possibilities are limitless. And when roles and responsibilities are aligned with individual skills, the business becomes a true reflection of the best that each partner or team member has to offer.

THE POWER OF PRIORITIZATION

As a business owner, decisions come at you in a never-ending stream. Often, this takes the form of constant incoming calls, each one demanding attention, each promising to be the most important. Effective leadership isn't about answering every call but knowing which ones to pick up and when to let others go to voicemail. This is where the power of prioritization comes into play.

Not all decisions are created equal. It's counterproductive—and quite frankly, impossible—to treat every decision as if it holds the same weight. Some decisions will have a significant impact on your business's trajectory while others might only affect the next hour. The hard part is discerning which is which.

When faced with a decision, we've found that discussing the options thoroughly and then making a clear yes-or-no choice is the most efficient way to move forward. The clarity of a yes-or-no decision is invaluable. A no today doesn't mean it can't become a yes in the future, but it allows us to stay focused on what truly matters in the present moment.

In fact, saying no is often more important than saying yes because it protects us from distractions. Every yes comes with a commitment of time, energy, and resources—commodities that are always in limited supply—so by learning to say no to what doesn't align with our core objectives, we ensure that every yes is meaningful and impactful.

But we recognize that saying no isn't easy, especially when you're trying to build and grow a new business. It can feel like you're closing the door on potential success. But in reality, saying no is about keeping doors open to the right opportunities. Every no today preserves the space for a yes tomorrow, so when you do commit, you can do so fully and with confidence.

When you prioritize effectively, the benefits ripple throughout the entire business. You're not just completing tasks; you're moving your business forward and aligning your actions with your long-term vision. Prioritization reduces stress, increases productivity, and enhances your ability to make strategic decisions.

It also fosters a sense of control and purpose. Rather than feeling overwhelmed by a never-ending to-do list, you can approach each day with clarity, knowing that you're working on the right things. This clarity isn't just good for the business, it's good for you personally. It allows you to end each day with a sense of accomplishment, knowing that your efforts are making a real difference.

Mastering the power of prioritization is an ongoing process that requires regular reflection, adjustment, and a continually renewed commitment to discipline. But the rewards are worth it. By prioritizing effectively, you can lead your business with intentionality and avoid the trap of being busy simply to be busy. Every decision, every action, and every moment counts. And when you align every decision with your goals and vision, you give yourself the greatest chance to grow, thrive, and succeed.

THE FOUR BUCKETS OF WORK

To streamline our decision-making and make sure that we're always focused on what truly matters, we use the Eisenhower Matrix (Figure 5) to categorize our work into four distinct buckets.

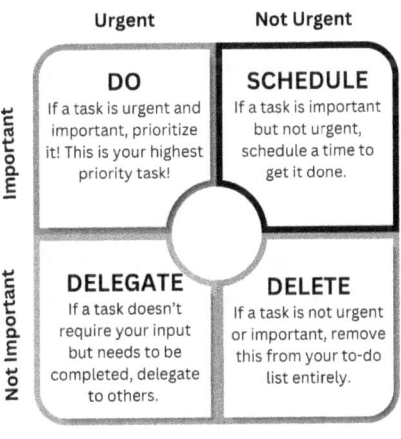

FIGURE 5

1. **Urgent and Important:** These tasks demand immediate attention and are crucial to our business's success. This may include pressing deadlines, client complaints, or preparing for an upcoming presentation. These are the highest priorities or fires that need to be put out first. Handling these tasks promptly ensures that the business continues to operate smoothly and that key relationships are maintained.

2. **Not Urgent but Important:** These tasks are important for our long-term success but don't require immediate action. Planning, professional development, and client relationship-building fall into this category. This bucket is often where the most strategic work happens—work that sets the foundation for future growth and stability.

   However, because these tasks aren't screaming for our attention, they can easily be overlooked or postponed indefinitely. So we make it a priority to tackle them as soon as the urgent and important tasks are completed. That way, we're not just putting out fires but also building a fireproof business.

3. **Urgent but Not Important:** These tasks need immediate attention but don't contribute to our long-term goals. Examples include proofreading draft documents, checking phone/email alerts, or dealing with unnecessary interruptions. It's easy to get caught up in these tasks because they often feel pressing. However, their urgency is deceptive, and they pull us away from more important work. To manage these tasks, we either delegate them or find ways to minimize their impact on our day.

4. **Not Urgent and Not Important:** These are the time-wasters—browsing the internet, watching TV, handling trivial to-dos—that contribute nothing to our business's success.

They are distractions, pure and simple. While it's important to take breaks and recharge, these activities should be limited and structured so they don't eat into productive time. More often than not, we deprioritize or eliminate these tasks entirely.

By categorizing our tasks into these four buckets, we can quickly identify where to direct our energy. We always start with the tasks in bucket one. Once those are completed, we move on to bucket two. This approach ensures that we're not just busy, but productive and focused on the work that truly advances our business.

Be aware, this kind of prioritization requires discipline. It's tempting to tackle the easy tasks first, to clear out the inbox or respond to every notification. But discipline means resisting that temptation and focusing on the tasks that matter most, even when they are difficult or time-consuming.

The discipline of focus also means being proactive rather than reactive. By prioritizing important but not urgent tasks, we prevent many urgent issues from arising in the first place. For example, by investing time in planning and professional development, we can avoid crises down the road and ensure that we're prepared to seize opportunities when they arise.

EVALUATING OPPORTUNITIES

The allure of new business offerings or projects can be powerful. Whether it's the promise of immediate revenue, the excitement of innovation, or the desire to stay ahead of the competition, the temptation to jump on every opportunity is real. Evaluating new opportunities requires more than just enthusiasm—it requires a methodical approach that allows you to assess the true value of each possibility.

In our business, we've developed a simple yet effective visual tool (Figure 6) that helps us do just that. This tool allows us to define the "what," "who," and "how" of each opportunity. What exactly are we considering? Who will be impacted or involved? And how does this align with our current strategy and resources? By answering these questions, we gain clarity on whether the opportunity is worth pursuing or if it's something that should be set aside.

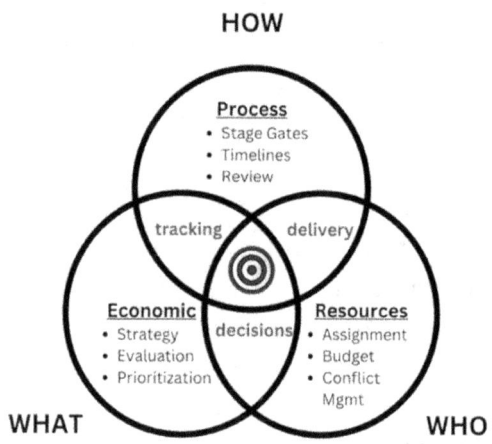

FIGURE 6

By mapping out the "what," "who," and "how," we can see not only the potential benefits but also the potential risks and challenges. This clarity often leads us to a surprising conclusion: The best decision might be to walk away. By "self-canceling" projects that don't meet our criteria, we avoid wasting time and resources on initiatives that won't ultimately advance our business.

This isn't about being overly cautious—it's about being strategic and intentional in our actions. This disciplined approach helps us avoid the common pitfall of spreading ourselves too thin and instead allows us to concentrate our efforts where they will have the most significant impact.

When you know that every project you take on is aligned with your business goals and has been carefully considered, you can work with confidence and clarity. There's no nagging doubt about whether you've made the right choice or whether you're wasting resources on a dead-end initiative.

This clarity also enhances productivity. By focusing on the projects and opportunities that matter most, you can allocate your time, energy, and resources more effectively. You're not just busy; you're productive in a way that moves your business forward. And because you've already weeded out the lower-value opportunities, you can give your full attention to the initiatives that have the greatest potential for success.

In the end, it's not about chasing every opportunity that comes your way—it's about choosing the right ones and executing them with excellence. By doing so, you position your business for sustainable growth and long-term success.

CHAPTER EIGHT
HIRING TOP TALENT

ONE OF THE MOST IMPORTANT decisions you will make for your business is when to hire your first team members. In the beginning, it was just you (and maybe your co-founder), but now you're bringing in an outsider, and that new person is going to make a big impact on your business—good or bad.

Before you dive into recruiting, regardless of the role or industry, you need to understand some of the common mistakes founders make so you can avoid them. These missteps can lead to costly setbacks and hinder your business's growth. In this chapter, we'll guide you through these common pitfalls and offer some practical strategies so you're fully prepared to hire successfully.

KNOWING WHEN TO HIRE

A big mistake we see founders make is deciding to hire without fully considering whether their company is truly ready. It's easy to feel like hiring is the next logical step, especially when you're stretched thin. However, just like any other significant business decision, hiring should never be done impulsively.

So first, ask yourself this question: *Do I know exactly **who** I need to hire and **why**?*

Maybe you want to step back from selling or leading projects and need an account executive or other contributor to take over, or perhaps your lead generation or project delivery metrics are lagging, and another person could be more efficient and effective in executing on the deliverables. Whatever the case, it's important to have a clear reason for each hire.

> **Timing** is another critical factor. While some founders hire quickly, others take months or even longer. Planning your hiring timeline in advance will ensure that the process starts at the right time to keep your business on track.
>
> **Budget** is also an important consideration. Hiring an A+ person can be transformative, but it involves some upfront costs that you need to be prepared for. Make sure you've done the math and have a budget that supports not just the hire but also the time it might take to see a return on that investment.

Also, attracting top talent isn't just about offering someone a job—it's about offering them a role within a company that they are excited to join. A+ talent wants to work for leaders who inspire, challenge, and support them, so if you haven't positioned yourself as a leader that top-tier candidates would want to work with, you might struggle to attract the right people.

This positioning requires more than just a strong business plan. You must be ready to lead effectively. You must be prepared with clear onboarding, playbooks, and processes to support your new hire from day one. If these aren't in place, now is the time to create them. Consider recording everything you do related to the role you want to hire for a week or two. This documentation will serve as a solid foundation for your onboarding materials and processes.

Being ready to lead also means making sure that whoever will manage the new employee is prepared, whether that will be you or someone else on your team.

KNOWING WHO TO HIRE

Hiring the wrong person for the wrong role is one of the most common mistakes founders make. To avoid this, you must have a clear understanding of who you need and why. Misalignment between the hire's role and your business needs can lead to inefficiencies and wasted resources.

For example, if you need someone to take over sales or project management, hiring a generalist might not be the best choice. Or if your primary need is lead generation, bringing in a closer could be a mismatch. Clearly define the role and its responsibilities before starting the hiring process so you can bring on someone who genuinely adds value to your business.

The checklist in Figure 7 summarizes all the things we recommend business owners do well in advance of posting a job opening. Use it to make sure you're ready to hire.

Hiring Checklist - Are YOU ready?

- You know exactly who you need to hire and why (who & why)
- You know when you want to hire (timeline)
- You have the budget
- You have onboarding, playbooks and processes in place

FIGURE 7

DOUBLING DOWN AS DUALPRENEURS

POSITIONING YOURSELF CORRECTLY AS A LEADER

Beyond knowing when and who to hire, there's an important part of the hiring process that often goes overlooked. Before you start trying to find the right candidate to meet your needs, you need to position yourself correctly as a leader.

As leaders, we focus so much on finding the best candidates that it's easy to forget those candidates are going to be evaluating us too. The best talent wants to work for the best companies with the best products and under the best leadership.

If you as a leader aren't prepared to lead or don't present yourself as a great leader with a cohesive, motivated team, the top candidates will likely lose interest in the opportunity and drop out of the process. This is where many leaders and companies get it wrong. They fail to consider their company from the candidates' perspective.

Today's interviewing and hiring environment is vastly different from what it was in the past. Now more than ever, you need to be someone that other people genuinely want to work with. It's not enough to simply find the best candidates; you must also be a leader with the qualities they admire. To attract and retain A+ talent, you need to sell top candidates on your leadership, your team, and your company just as much as they need to sell themselves to you. It's a reciprocal process.

Before you start hiring, make sure your story and leadership style are compelling enough to amaze potential hires. Are you presenting yourself as the kind of leader who inspires confidence and excitement? If not, it's time to refine your approach.

How often do you share your company's mission, vision, and core values during the interview process? If you aren't talking about these things passionately and frequently, you're missing a perfect opportunity to connect with candidates on a deeper level.

The rest of your team should be just as obsessed with these values as you are, and this should be evident during every interaction they have with potential hires. If no one on your team is teasing you for how often you bring up these topics, you're probably not mentioning them enough.

It's also worth noting that some of the best candidates will reach out to your current team members before the interview. They'll want to get a sense of what it's really like to work for you and your company. If they don't like what they hear, they might decide not to show up at all.

So make sure your entire team embodies the values and culture you've worked to create. Everyone should be on the same page and ready to present a unified, positive image of your leadership and the company.

You need to actively showcase your leadership if you want to attract and retain the best talent. By aligning your leadership style with the expectations of top candidates, sharing your mission and values with passion, and making sure your team reflects these values, you will position your company as a place where the best talent wants to be.

Six Qualities of a Leader That A+ Players Want to Follow

Through extensive research and screening thousands of candidates over the years, we've identified six key qualities (Figure 8) that consistently stand out as essential for leaders who want to attract and retain top-tier talent. These qualities are not just desirable—they are necessary for inspiring confidence and loyalty in the best players.

Visionary & Strategic	Supportive & Empowering	Transparent & Honest
Experienced & Knowledgeable	Motivational & Inspiring	Accessible & Approachable

FIGURE 8

1. Visionary and Strategic

A visionary and strategic leader has a clear picture of where the company is headed and how to get there. They inspire their team by communicating a compelling vision for the future and crafting strategies that align with long-term goals. This isn't about having lofty ideas without substance; it's about having a realistic, data-driven plan that guides the team through change and innovation.

I (Angie) once worked with a leader like this. He consistently communicated his vision to the team, and he made sure everyone understood the direction and their role within it. He avoided shiny object syndrome—getting distracted by every new trend—because he used data and thorough research before introducing any new initiatives. His strategic approach made the whole team feel confident and focused because we knew we were part of something meaningful. We would have followed him anywhere.

Candidates need to see this visionary quality in you from the beginning, so articulate your vision clearly during the interview process.

2. Supportive and Empowering

A supportive and empowering leader provides their team with the resources, tools, and encouragement they need to succeed. They trust their team members to take ownership of their roles and make decisions, only stepping in to guide when it's necessary. This type of leader creates an environment where people feel valued and capable.

Imagine a leader who, when a team member comes up with a new idea, encourages them to pursue it and provides the necessary resources. They offer guidance and support but let the team member take the lead. This approach not only encourages innovation but also builds trust and confidence within the team.

During an interview, this kind of supportive and empowering attitude must shine through. Candidates want to know that they will be given the autonomy to excel in their role while having the support they need to succeed.

3. Transparent and Honest

Transparency and honesty are foundational for building trust within a team. A transparent leader communicates openly about both successes and challenges in order to create a culture of respect and integrity. The leader doesn't shy away from difficult conversations and believes in sharing information, even when the news isn't positive.

For example, consider a leader who, during a tough quarter, holds a meeting with the team to discuss the challenges openly. They share the company's financial situation, the reasons behind the struggles, and their plan to turn things around. This level of honesty helps the team understand the situation and rally together to overcome the obstacles.

Candidates want to know that you are the type of leader who will be straightforward with them. Personally, we strongly discourage the all-too-common "shit sandwich" approach where bad news is sandwiched between two layers of insincere praise. Instead, we advocate for being clear and honest about what's going well and what needs to improve.

4. Experienced and Knowledgeable

Experience and knowledge are both non negotiable for a leader. A leader who deeply understands the industry, market, and intricacies of their business can offer valuable insights and practical solutions to challenges. A+ candidates are looking for a leader they can learn from, someone who knows the ropes and can guide them effectively. Leaders who lack this depth of knowledge will struggle to earn the respect of top talent.

5. Motivational and Inspiring

A motivational and inspiring leader has the ability to energize and uplift their team. This is about more than cheerleading. Rather, it's about leading by example. It's about demonstrating passion for and commitment to the company's goals. Such leaders recognize and celebrate achievements and keep the team motivated and driven to excel.

In every interview, you need to showcase your ability to inspire and motivate. Candidates want to see that you're not just looking for someone to fill a role but that you're passionate about the company's mission and excited about the journey ahead.

6. Accessible and Approachable

Although often overlooked, accessibility and approachability are two important qualities that any great leader should possess. An accessible leader encourages open communication and makes it easy for team members to come forward with their ideas, concerns, or questions by creating a welcoming environment where everyone feels heard and valued.

For example, we had a top candidate back out of a hiring process because of an accessibility red flag. He asked each of the first three interviewers about the communication loop and how accessible the CEO was since he would be reporting to her. Each interviewer told him that communication was mostly chaotic and that they rarely had access to the CEO. They also admitted that the CEO often canceled meetings at the last minute. Before even reaching the final interview with the CEO, the candidate withdrew because he didn't feel he would have the support he needed.

To attract top talent, you must demonstrate that you are accessible and approachable, that your team has an open line of communication to you. Candidates want to know that when they join your company, they will have the support and guidance they need without barriers.

THE PERFECT CANDIDATE

OK, now that you've started working on making yourself the kind of leader that top talent wants to work for, it's time to consider the qualities of the perfect candidate. Remember, building a successful team isn't just about filling positions. It's about finding the right people who will drive your business forward. That means you need to know exactly who you're looking for.

When you have a clear picture of your ideal candidate, you can target your recruiting efforts more effectively, which will make the hiring process more efficient. With clarity, you can quickly identify the right fit and move past those who don't align with your needs.

Moreover, when you know exactly what you're looking for, you're more likely to find someone who not only meets the job requirements but also fits well with your company's culture. This will give you a higher success rate in hiring and a smoother process of integrating the new hire into your team.

So how do you figure out what you're looking for? Let's explore how you can define the traits, skills, and values of your ideal candidate. First, we recommend focusing on three key categories:

Vision, Values, and Velocity. Each of these categories encompasses the critical qualities that define an A+ candidate.

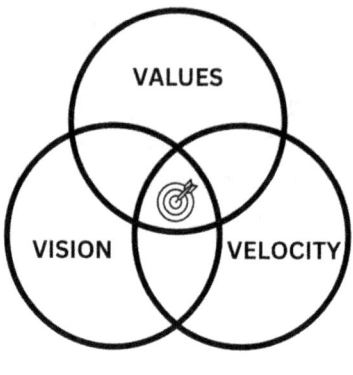

FIGURE 9

Vision

An A+ candidate should have a clear vision for their career that aligns with your company's strategic goals. They should set ambitious yet realistic goals and demonstrate a strong desire for continuous learning and self-improvement. You want someone who brings fresh ideas and is willing to challenge the status quo, a candidate who shows leadership potential even if they're not in a leadership role yet. They should also be adaptable to change and willing to adjust their vision and strategies as necessary to align with evolving business needs.

Values

Values are the foundation of a candidate's character and reveal how well they will fit within your team and company culture. A candidate with the right values will be a strong cultural fit who exhibits a solid work ethic, integrity, and a commitment to your company's mission. They will take accountability seriously, consistently deliver on their commitments, and demonstrate passion in their work. When a candidate's values align with those of your company, they're not just looking for a job. They're looking to make a meaningful contribution to a shared vision.

Velocity

Velocity refers to a candidate's ability to deliver results efficiently and effectively. The perfect candidate is process-driven and has a well-defined approach to their work that consistently yields results. They are adaptable, able to pivot when needed, and focused on achieving measurable outcomes. They are high achievers with a proven track record of success who are adept at managing their time and prioritizing tasks to meet deadlines and drive the business forward.

By focusing on Vision, Values, and Velocity in your hiring decisions, you greatly increase the chances that your next employee will be a true asset to your team and company. By defining these qualities before you begin the hiring process, you can streamline your efforts, increase your success rate, and ultimately build a stronger, more cohesive team.

Ideally, an A+ candidate should possess all three of these qualities. A person with Vision and Values but not Velocity isn't a top performer. Neither is someone with Velocity and Values but not Vision. Look for someone who possesses all three.

Take the time to build out what these three categories look like specifically for your team. Define the traits, skills, and values that align with your company's goals and culture. This will guide you in finding and hiring the perfect candidates.

THE COMPLETE HIRING PROCESS

Now, with that in mind, let's take a look at the entire hiring process. This is such a big decision for your business that we want to walk you through the whole process—from defining the ideal candidate to making an offer and keeping them engaged until they start.

Figure 10 shows all five steps of the complete hiring process. Let's walk through them one at a time.

FIGURE 10

Step 1: Define Your Ideal Hire and Craft a Job Description

The first step in the hiring process is to clearly define who you're looking for. That means identifying key traits, skills, and cultural fit as well as setting clear objectives for the role.

Start by listing the nonnegotiable qualities your ideal candidate *must* possess, such as work ethic, resilience, and adaptability. Next, determine the specific skills and experience necessary for the role—whether it's industry knowledge or technical proficiency with sales tools. Equally important is the cultural fit: What type of personality will thrive in your company's environment? Think about your team dynamics and the values that are vital to your organization.

Then, set clear objectives for what you expect this hire to achieve. For example, if the role involves hitting a million-dollar quota with an average deal size of $85,000, make sure the candidate has experience managing similar targets.

Once you've defined these criteria, craft a detailed job description that includes all the traits, skills, experience, and cultural fit elements. Be specific and comprehensive. Clearly outline the must-haves, nice-to-haves, and knockout criteria.

Step 2: Targeted Recruiting

With a clear candidate profile, your next step is to execute a targeted recruiting strategy. Knowing exactly what you're looking for allows you to narrow your search and avoid wasting time on unsuitable candidates.

Leverage tools like LinkedIn Sales Navigator to identify potential candidates based on the key traits and skills you've defined. Look for signs of recent company changes such as layoffs, leadership shifts, or acquisitions that might make a candidate more open to new opportunities. Tap into your network and encourage referrals as these often yield high-quality candidates.

Be strategic with job ads. Instead of blasting ads absolutely everywhere, which will only dilute your brand and make it seem like you're desperate, focus on targeted outreach. If you're working with a recruiting firm, consider partnering with just one trusted firm that can represent your company well. Ideally, your recruiting efforts should be discreet and make top candidates feel like they're part of an exclusive process.

Step 3: Efficiency and Preparation

Efficiency in the hiring process is important, and preparation is how you achieve it. Get your current top performers and other stakeholders involved in the process. Their input can provide valuable insights and help you refine your criteria based on new trends or changing business needs.

Make sure your interview process is well-organized and that everyone involved is prepared. Share the process with candidates upfront so they know what to expect. Prepare for interviews with the same diligence you would apply to presenting to investors. If you're using a recruiting agency, run your process by them for feedback and suggestions.

Figure 11 is one simple example of how one of our clients prepares for interviews. As they are planning in a group setting, they have each team member fill this out based on what was previously discussed. This way, everyone is on the same page and following the same process.

PREPARING FOR THE INITIAL INTERVIEW

During this stage, you'll assign the interviewer and clarify their role. Focus on defining the specific skills to seek in candidates, establish a scoring system to assess their fit, and select the interview questions. Be sure to outline the ideal timeline for candidate progression and identify relevant KPIs to track progress.

Who

Role

Scoring (1-5 scale) What is your interviewer looking for?

Timing How long does it take to move from one stage to the next?

KPIs

Questions Choose up to 10-15 questions that strongly resonate with you and align with the specific type of interview you want to conduct.

FIGURE 11

Step 4: Conducting Interviews

The purpose of an interview is to assess whether a candidate truly fits the profile you've created. Develop targeted interview questions that will uncover the traits, skills, and cultural fit you're looking for. Include some scenarios and role-playing exercises to see how candidates perform in real-life situations.

Communication is important during the interview process, so keep candidates informed at every step. Keep your recruiting firm (if you're using one) equally in the loop. Always be punctual for interviews. Remember, candidates are evaluating you just as much as you're evaluating them. Missing or being late for an interview is a major red flag that can deter top talent.

Give candidates plenty of time to ask their own questions during the interview. This is their opportunity for them to assess whether your company is the right fit for them, so give them more than just a few minutes to voice their concerns or curiosities.

If you find the right candidate, move quickly! While it's important not to cut corners, you should progress through the process efficiently. The longer you wait, the more likely it is that another company will swoop in and make an offer. If you're confident in a candidate, don't wait for other candidates to show up to compare them to. That will prove to be a waste of everyone's time. Go ahead and make them an offer. Conversely, if a candidate isn't right for the role, let them know promptly and provide specific feedback.

Step 5: Making the Offer

When it comes time to make an offer, practice transparency and fairness. Stick to what was discussed during the interview process. Never try to undercut the agreed-upon terms. A fair, straightforward offer will leave little room for counteroffers, and it builds trust from the start.

Always call the candidate with the offer before sending it via email. This personal touch allows you to address any questions or concerns they may have before they see the formal offer letter. Once the offer is sent, give the candidate no more than seventy-two hours to accept unless there's a good reason for a longer deliberation period. This urgency helps prevent the candidate from shopping the offer around to other potential employers.

Once the offer is accepted, maintain frequent contact with the candidate until they start. Keep the communication lines open. That means inviting them to team events, taking them to lunch, and including them in virtual meetings. This helps them feel welcomed and engaged, and it reduces the risk of them accepting another offer elsewhere. If you plan to send company swag, do so as soon as the offer is accepted. Also, have everyone involved in the interview process send a personalized welcome email.

Remember, a positive experience during the hiring process makes it much harder for candidates to entertain other offers. Keep them top of mind from the moment they accept your offer through their first day on the job and onwards!

CHAPTER NINE

THE POWER OF PROMOTION

IT'S NO LONGER ENOUGH TO offer a great product or service. In today's fast-paced and hyper-connected world, you have to get the word out about your business in smart, targeted, and creative ways. The problem is, with so many options—including social media, podcasts, blogs, and in-person events—it can be overwhelming to know where to start or what's effective.

More than ever, you have to be strategic in how you approach marketing and content creation so you know you are consistently reaching the right people with the right message. The key to making marketing work for you is to have a well-rounded and multifaceted approach. Social media platforms, podcasts, blogs, and email campaigns each serve a specific purpose, but the common thread through them all is engagement. Your audience needs to feel connected to your brand, and you encourage that connection by sharing authentic, valuable content.

In other words, **content is king.** By consistently creating valuable content that informs, entertains, or solves a problem for your target audience, you will set yourself up as a thought leader in your industry. Share insights, address common challenges that you know your target audience deals with, and offer new perspectives. This kind of regular content production builds authority, trust, and engagement over time and positions you and your business as go-to resources in your field.

However, it's not enough to just create content. You also need a solid **social media strategy** that will put your content in front of the right audience. Individual platforms cater to different demographics and communication styles, so it's important to know which one is right for you.

For example, LinkedIn is ideal for reaching professionals and decision-makers while Instagram and X (formerly Twitter) are better suited for a broader, more casual audience. Figure out where your audience spends the most time and tailor your approach accordingly. That is how you optimize engagement and build a strong online presence.

Finally, to maximize your online impact, you can **repurpose your content** across multiple channels. A single blog post can be broken down into short, digestible social media snippets or serve as the topic for a podcast episode. By repackaging important ideas in a variety of formats, you will reach a wider audience without having to reinvent the wheel, which will make your content creation efforts more efficient and impactful.

We also recommend creating a **social media calendar** to help you stay consistent. Tools like Canva are great for designing visually appealing posts, and scheduling tools allow you to automate weeks or even months of content at a time.

THE POWER OF PROMOTION

FROM OCEAN TO POND

When you first start posting online, it can feel like you're casting your net into a vast ocean, hoping to catch any little fish that swims along. You just want to reach anyone who may be interested in your product or service. However, effective marketing requires narrowing your focus and targeting specific people. It's more like fishing in a well-stocked pond.

So instead of trying to appeal to everyone, concentrate on a niche market that needs what you're offering. Sounds simple enough, but how do you identify your target audience? Basic demographic information isn't enough. We encourage you to dive deep into the behaviors, pain points, and desires of the people who need the solution you offer. Who are these people? Where do they spend their time, and what are they looking for?

The more specific you can get in defining your audience, the better equipped you'll be to create content that truly resonates with them. You will be able to connect with them on a deeper level by addressing their specific needs and building a relationship based on trust and value.

Once you've clearly defined your audience, your next priority is to develop targeted outreach. Again, don't try to cast your net too widely. Instead, focus on the channels where your audience is most active. LinkedIn and other social media platforms allow you to hone your content to the exact people who fit your target profile so you can tailor your message directly to their needs and interests. Clear, relevant messages will lead to stronger engagement and a more effective connection.

DOUBLING DOWN AS DUALPRENEURS

CRAFTING THE PERFECT PITCH

If you're going to market your business effectively, you also have to practice the art of creating a compelling pitch. Remember, a pitch is really about how you solve problems for your ideal customer. It needs to be clear, concise, and—most importantly—relevant to the listener.

Personalization is important if you want to connect with your target audience, so tailor your message to people you want to reach, whether they're potential investors, customers, or partners. Each group has different priorities and concerns, so a one-size-fits-all approach won't cut it.

For example, a pitch to an investor should focus on financial projections and growth potential while a pitch to a customer should emphasize the product's benefits and how it solves their specific problems. Once you understand your audience's unique perspective, you can deliver a more compelling and relevant message that speaks directly to their needs.

It's also incredibly important to convey the value that your business, product, or service brings to the table. Center your pitch on how you can solve problems or add meaningful value to your audience's life or business. Don't just list a bunch of features or capabilities. Instead, focus on their needs and how your solution addresses those needs. Position your business as the answer to your ideal customer's challenges. In doing so, you create a stronger connection and a more persuasive pitch.

One tried-and-true technique is the **elevator pitch**, which goes like this: If you had just one minute to explain your business to someone in an elevator, what would you say to spark interest and leave them wanting more?

Our elevator pitch for Done!, LLC is, "We help small businesses with project management consulting, training, coaching, and ad hoc project delivery." For GSD Coach & Recruiting, it's "We help B2B SaaS companies hire the top five percent of sales talent . . . *fast!*"

NETWORKING IS YOUR BACKBONE

Networking is the foundation of any strategy for getting the word out about your business. Remember, it's not just *what* you know but *who* you know. More importantly, it's about who knows you.

Networking and building relationships take time and effort, but the rewards are tremendous. The challenge is that these skills don't come naturally to everyone. Travis has always been a consummate networker, but Angie needed to bolster her networking skills. So if you're not already great at it, you're not alone. But here's the good news: It's never too late to improve.

As we said before, when you're running a business, it's all about relationships, and these relationships need to extend beyond your immediate circle. So get comfortable connecting with people at a higher level, even if they're outside of your team, division, or company.

Chances are, what got you to this point in your business has been your ability to "do." But if you want to keep moving forward, you have to start focusing on "knowing" and "connecting." You need to become a strategic partner and thinker, not just a doer who completes tasks, because it's key relationships that are going to keep your business growing.

DOUBLING DOWN AS DUALPRENEURS

FROM DOING TO CONNECTING

Remember, success is not the result of being busy and doing as much as you can. Rather, it is the result of focusing on doing only those things that move you forward. To that end, the relationships you build can open doors to new opportunities, partnerships, and growth.

Attending in-person events can keep your network fresh, relevant, and growing, so make time for in-person conferences—like the SaaS Academy, Project Management Institute, or Scaled Agile Framework events—on a regular basis to forge new relationships. The power of face-to-face interactions cannot be overstated.

In addition to traditional networking, there are several other ways to get the word out about your business and create valuable connections.

- **Podcasts and Blogs:** These platforms offer you a chance to showcase your expertise while engaging with a broader audience. Partner with other people in your industry to reach new potential clients.
- **In-Person Training/Lunch & Learns:** These kinds of events provide hands-on experiences that allow for deeper connections with participants.
- **Online Training:** A scalable way to teach and engage with your audience.
- **Websites and Social Proof:** Make sure your website prominently features logos from well-known partners and clients. Social proof is a powerful trust-builder.

THE POWER OF PROMOTION

MAKING THE MOST OF SOCIAL MEDIA

Social media is still a cornerstone for business visibility but only if you're using the right platforms in the right ways. Here are some ways we leverage social media:

- **LinkedIn:** Perfect for professional connections, job postings, and thought leadership. Share insights, updates, and articles to maintain visibility in your network.
- **Facebook and Instagram:** Great for building a more casual, community-oriented presence.
- **X (formerly Twitter):** Best for timely updates, thought leadership, and connecting with influencers.

We also use **Canva** to design our posts, and we schedule them well in advance to ensure we maintain a consistent online presence.

Ultimately, getting the word out about your business requires more than just a solid marketing plan. You have to build relationships and leverage those connections strategically. Whether you're attending conferences, starting a podcast, or posting daily on LinkedIn, remember that the relationships you create (both in-person and online) will serve as the foundation of your long-term success.

Networking doesn't come naturally to everyone, but it's a skill anyone can develop. With plenty of practice, you can build the confidence to connect with people anywhere. The more you network, the more doors you will open for your business, so keep at it.

CHAPTER TEN

WAYS OF WORKING

GROWING A BUSINESS FROM A small startup to a large global enterprise is a journey that is full of challenges and opportunities. However, as you grow, the way you work will necessarily change.

At first glance, a small startup and a large global enterprise might seem worlds apart, but upon closer examination, they share some fundamental principles. Understanding the differences and similarities between the two can help you navigate your own business growth, whether you're just starting out or scaling up. Remember, we found much success by taking the lessons we learned from our corporate roles and experiences and applying them to our two businesses.

In a startup, everything is hands-on. As the founder, you are probably wearing multiple hats: founder, sales leader, marketing strategist, customer support, project manager, and even accountant. At this early stage, agility is of the utmost importance. Fortunately, you have the ability to pivot quickly and experiment without all the red tape that often comes with a larger organization. This flexibility can be a major advantage, especially when you're exploring new markets, testing products, or refining your service offerings.

DOUBLING DOWN AS DUALPRENEURS

As your business grows, your processes and structures need to evolve as well. What worked when you were small may not scale well. Now, you're going to need a defined organizational chart, clear communication channels, and standardized operating procedures if you want to maintain quality and efficiency. A growing business also requires an increasing focus on long-term vision and strategy.

This transition from the hustle of startup life to the operational sophistication of a large company is tricky, but it's necessary for sustainable growth.

However, there is one important similarity between startups and global enterprises: the need for innovation. Whether you're a scrappy startup or a billion-dollar corporation, innovation fuels your growth. For startups, this often means quick iteration and experimentation. Personally, we've found that regularly stepping back and reassessing our ways of working helps us experiment with new ideas quickly and make decisions on a timely basis—something we could not do as readily in the corporate world.

In large companies, innovation is almost always slower, but it is still important to stay competitive in a changing market. Regardless of your business's size, you need to continuously adapt and evolve to thrive.

GROWING A BUSINESS WITHOUT EMPLOYEES

Earlier in this book, we gave you a process of identifying, recruiting, and retaining employees. But we also pointed out that we run both of our businesses without any employees. It's just the two of us, and for the foreseeable future, it will stay that way. Maybe that sounds appealing to you.

In fact, many entrepreneurs ask us questions like, "Is it possible to run and grow a business efficiently without employees?" The answer is yes but with caveats. Running a business without employees means being strategic about leveraging resources like automation, outsourcing, and technology.

There's an array of technology tools these days that can help streamline processes and do all sorts of tasks for you. You need to take advantage of these tools because there's a limit to how much you can scale alone. Automation tools such as CRM systems, scheduling apps (e.g., Calendly), video conferencing platforms (e.g., Zoom, MS Teams, and Google Meet), and accounting software (e.g., QuickBooks) can significantly reduce the amount of work you have to do.

Many solo (or duo) entrepreneurs also rely on outsourcing to optimize their time so they can focus on growth. You can outsource tasks like bookkeeping, marketing, or administrative work, which will save you from a lot of time-consuming, day-to-day operational tasks. This frees you up to dedicate most of your energy to high-level strategy and decision-making.

By combining outsourcing and smart technology, you can maintain your productivity and drive growth without getting bogged down by everyday tasks. Still, without employees, scaling your business will likely take longer. After all, your time is limited, and to grow, you may eventually need to bring on help.

Whether it's hiring employees or working with contractors, having other people take on tasks that fall outside your core competencies will help push your business forward. We love to form strategic and practical partnerships with other experts to help us expand what we can offer to our clients.

DOUBLING DOWN AS DUALPRENEURS

KNOW YOUR STRENGTHS AND WEAKNESSES

Beyond getting help and leveraging tools for menial work and daily tasks, you also need to know your own strengths and weaknesses so you can maximize your own impact and efficiency. In our own journey as dualpreneurs, we learned the value of clearly defining our roles and responsibilities (as discussed in Chapter Seven). The distinctions between our individual roles have been essential to our success, but we didn't arrive at them by accident.

We conducted a thorough audit of the work each of us was doing, identified which tasks we each wanted to keep, which we wanted to transfer, and which we needed to stop doing. This process allowed us to create roles in which we waste as little effort as possible and focus on areas where we each have both competence and interest—the activities we love that keep us focused, energized, and happy.

Our philosophy is simple: If you can't do something with love, why do it at all?

By knowing your strengths and weaknesses, you can focus on the things that you are best at and transfer the rest to someone else (or to outside resources). This isn't just about being more efficient. It's also about finding peace of mind and joy in your work.

Now, if you're dualpreneurs like us, then a lot of your peace of mind is going to hinge on the quality of the working relationship between the two of you. Divvying up the roles and responsibilities correctly certainly contributes to this relationship, but even then, conflict is inevitable in business.

WAYS OF WORKING

CONFLICT RESOLUTION IN PRACTICE

Running a business with a partner is going to bring conflict sooner or later, but that's OK! You just have to learn how to deal with disagreements in a healthy way. Personally, we've learned that you can say whatever you want as long as you say it with respect. Everyone wants to feel like their self-worth is protected, so healthy conflict resolution starts by recognizing that *every* voice deserves to be heard.

Let's face it. With any new business venture, setbacks and failures are going to happen. It's part of the process of growing a business, so it's something you have to embrace. As Winston Churchill said, "Success consists of going from failure to failure without loss of enthusiasm."[6] It's important to keep this in mind when you start or scale your business, but it's *especially* important when two joint owners are involved.

Ideally, you learn from each setback, but you also need a healthy way of dealing with them as joint owners. In fact, any business owner would be well-served to learn how to resolve conflict.

Early on in our own partnership, one of us didn't like conflict and often pushed uncomfortable conversations to the side, but we've since learned that sharing personal life and business life means conflict is most certainly unavoidable. When it happens, we need to address it head-on.

So now, we take a proactive approach. When there's conflict, we talk about it *right away*. It might take a few conversations to fully resolve the issue, but our goal is to be aligned in the end.

We've also learned that we can't solve problems for each other. We don't live in each other's reality, so each of us needs a voice at the table to express our own perspective. To that end, we've created "Walking 1:1s," a time during which we take walks together while talking through issues openly and calmly. During these walks, we check in with each other by asking, "Where are we at with this? Do we need more info, or can we make a decision now?"

Conflict Resolution Tactics

1. **Stick to the facts** and take a tactical approach.

2. **Be brave and bold**; don't cower from doing what is necessary.

3. **Say what needs to be said**—but remember, less is more.

4. **Be respectful** and keep your shared values in mind.

5. **Remember that disagreement isn't personal.**

6. **Praise in public, criticize in private.**

7. **Find common ground** before offering alternative perspectives and suggestions.

8. **Leave room for other viewpoints.** Disagreements can result from narrow-mindedness.

9. **Respond thoughtfully instead of reacting.** Breathe, think, listen, and then talk.

10. Keep in mind this wisdom from author Josh McDowell: **"It is more rewarding to resolve a conflict than to dissolve a relationship."**[7]

Conflict is natural and normal in any business partnership, and it can be healthy as long as you address it head-on, listen with empathy, and work together toward resolution.

The fact is, running a business, whether it's a small startup or a large enterprise, comes with its own unique challenges. But regardless of the size of your business, some principles remain constant: You need to know your strengths, prioritize your time, communicate openly, and embrace conflict as an opportunity for growth. Growth requires change, and change often brings discomfort, but that's where innovation, progress, and success converge.

CHAPTER ELEVEN

PROJECT MANAGEMENT

PROJECT MANAGEMENT IS ONE OF those skills you're going to have to master, no matter the size of your business or your industry or the title you hold. We're talking about far more than simply tracking timelines, budgets, or deliverables. Good project management is about being adaptable, understanding your client's needs, and executing solutions that work. To do that well, you will have to master four skills: **listening, sales, consulting,** and **process improvement**.

LISTENING WELL

First, great project managers are great listeners. In fact, listening is arguably the most important skill in project management. Why? Because every project begins with understanding the needs, challenges, and goals of stakeholders, whether they are clients, team members, or partners. Listening allows you to absorb valuable information and uncover the root of a problem before you jump to a solution.

DOUBLING DOWN AS DUALPRENEURS

When managing a project, your ability to listen closely to clients and team members ensures that you are aligned with their expectations. This, in turn, helps you:

- Identify pain points early.
- Avoid miscommunication.
- Build stronger relationships.
- Gain a deeper understanding of the project scope.

Most issues that arise during a project can be traced back to a lack of understanding. By sharpening your listening skills, you will be better equipped to solve problems before they escalate.

Listening well is key to our Client Intake Process, which provides us with a thorough understanding of client requirements before we even begin a project. By taking the time to ask the right questions upfront, we can tailor our efforts to meet specific goals, align with expectations, and ultimately deliver better results.

Figures 12, 13, and 14 are templates we use when bringing on new recruiting clients, which we also tweak for our project consulting clients. They are designed to streamline communication and ensure every engagement starts on the right foot. You can use and modify any of these to suit your business.

PROJECT MANAGEMENT

For a Recruiting Client
General Info to Obtain or Ask

Company name and website
Primary contact name(s) and contact information (email and phone number)
Name and email of who we send the invoice to
Industry
Company address
How long in business
Primary product/service they are selling
Number of employees
Number of people on the sales team and what roles
Annual revenue
Anything else that we should know about the company that would get candidates excited about the role and the company

FIGURE 12

For a Recruiting Client
Compensation, Sales Metrics

Specific roles they are looking for
Location—remote or in the office—State specific? Anywhere in the US? Canada?
Who does this role report to? LI profile, email and phone #
High/low compensation range
Flexible compensation for the right candidate?
Walk through high level comp plan
Quota/is there a ramp period?
Average dollar amount of sale
Average length of sales (sales cycle duration)
Amount of travel-explain
Sales tools and tech
# of people needed to hire
Must have, like to have, knockouts (knockouts meaning that you absolutely don't want X)

FIGURE 13

PROJECT MANAGEMENT

For a Recruiting Client
Interview Process, Communication Style

Job description link or bullets if no JD Sections: About Us, Core Values, Role Overview, Responsibilities, Qualifications, Benefits
Timing of filling role(s)
What does the interview process look like (how many steps)
What is the turnaround time once we have submitted a candidate?
How will you communicate with me about the candidates I've submitted?
Who are all the people involved in the interview process? Provide scheduling links
Core values & company culture
What are all of the benefits?
What does the onboarding/ training process look like?
Who are the key competitors you would like us to source candidates from? Any companies that you would not like us to source from?
Share profiles of top sale representatives
Weekly communication preference? Email, 30 min meeting?

FIGURE 14

DOUBLING DOWN AS DUALPRENEURS

THE ART OF SALES

When people think about project management, sales isn't always a skill that comes to mind, but it should be. After all, to succeed as a project manager, you need to be able to sell your ideas, plans, and solutions to both your clients and your team. Sales is not just about selling a product but gaining buy-in, convincing others of the best course of action, and making sure that everyone is on board with the plan.

Project managers constantly "sell" in different ways.

Selling solutions to clients: Once you've identified a client's problem, you have to present your proposed solution in a way that makes them feel confident about your ability to deliver. We do this for both of our businesses by creating crisp, clear statements of work that outline the problem to solve, what we will deliver to solve the problem (with specific milestones and artifacts), the investment the client will make in that outcome, and simple pricing.

Selling ideas to stakeholders: Whether it's a new tool, methodology, or a change in process, getting everyone to buy into a new direction is necessary for smooth project execution. For our businesses, we create, compare, and contrast frameworks that show the pros and cons of our proposal. We give this to our clients and stakeholders as a pre-read, and we then schedule a follow-up meeting (more than one meeting may be required for large proposals). We also document all discussions, decisions, action items, owners, and next steps.

Selling the team on a vision: Your team needs to feel motivated and aligned with the project's goals, and it's your job to communicate that vision and rally everyone behind it. Even though it's just the two of us on our team, we share our thoughts on all proposals with any partners we've asked to get involved. That way, they have a voice at the table. It must be a win-win situation for all of us: our clients, our stakeholders, our partners, and our team.

Your ability to sell is incredibly important because, in the end, projects are about people. It's not enough to have a solid project plan. You also need to get other people to believe in it, support it, and act on it. Project management is the glue that holds everything else together!

PUTTING ON THE CONSULTING HAT

As a project manager, you also need to step into the role of a consultant. Clients will sometimes come to you with a general idea of what they want, but it's up to you to figure out the specifics and offer strategic guidance for achieving it. That means you have to be able to analyze the problem, provide a tailored solution, and advise the client on the best path forward.

The consulting mindset is about three things: **problem solving, adapting**, and **being proactive.**

First, the consulting mindset is about problem-solving, which means thoroughly understanding a client's true needs and then crafting actionable plans to address those needs. You must be able to analyze the surface issues while also identifying the underlying problems so you can provide an effective and lasting solution.

DOUBLING DOWN AS DUALPRENEURS

In our businesses, whether we're recruiting to fill a role or being brought in to manage a complex project or solve a problem, we've found that we both have a love for digging into the details to assess the current state and look at different options for delivering a successful outcome.

Adaptability is also incredibly important, since consulting often requires that you adjust to a wide variety of industries, client types, and project scopes. You must learn to be flexible and quick to grasp new environments so you can deliver value regardless of the unique circumstances you face.

We've found that we absolutely love to understand our clients' businesses, industries, and needs. Because of our diverse roles in the corporate world, we are able to quickly pivot our approach and ways of working to ensure client happiness and success. Our natural curiosity helps us to serve our clients by adapting how we learn and work with them.

Finally, a proactive approach is an essential element for any successful consultant. That means learning to anticipate challenges and offer solutions *before* the client even realizes there's a problem. This kind of foresight enables you to stay ahead and position yourself as a trusted advisor who drives continuous improvement and innovation.

This is where the combination of listening, establishing relationships, and being inquisitive brings out the best for clients. After we've listened and considered the best options to proceed, we often also identify other potential challenges or areas needing improvement that could be addressed concurrently. Our clients value that thoughtfulness and open approach to helping them.

Remember, consulting is about more than just managing tasks. It's about adding value and becoming a trusted advisor to your clients, an expert who helps them make informed decisions that will move their business forward.

PROJECT MANAGEMENT

IMPROVING PROCESSES

Ultimately, in order to be successful in any business or industry, you need to develop strong process improvement skills. A good book on this subject is *212° the Extra Degree: How to Achieve Results Beyond Your Wildest Expectations* by Sam Parker. We've both read it many, many times and have recommended it to leaders and teams throughout our careers.

The book provides a powerful guiding framework during times of change and transformation. It's loaded with valuable lessons that we've applied to project management, sales recruiting, and leadership. We encourage you to check it out. Here are a few of our favorite takeaways from the book:

The Extra Degree Makes the Difference

"At 211 degrees, water is hot. At 212 degrees, it boils. And with boiling water, comes steam. And with steam, you can power a train."[8] This is a great reminder that sometimes the smallest extra effort can lead to massive results.

In project management, going the extra mile, whether through communication, thoroughness, or problem-solving, can mean the difference between failure and success.

Persistence Is Key

Continued action and the application of heat (effort) to a task will achieve the objective you seek. Even in the most challenging phases of a project, persistence and focus are what get you across the finish line. We like to remind ourselves, "What you think about you bring about,"[9] to keep that positive focus and drive going during the more difficult times of an engagement.

DOUBLING DOWN AS DUALPRENEURS

The Line Between Success and Failure Is Thin

As American writer, publisher, and philosopher Elbert Hubbard put it, "The line between failure and success is so fine that we scarcely know when we pass it, so fine that we are often on the line and do not know it."[10] In other words, projects often fail because someone gave up just before a breakthrough. A little more effort, and what seemed like a hopeless situation could have been transformed into a success.

Successful project management requires constantly reviewing and refining processes. To that end, we have what we call Management Fix-It periods throughout the year where we review our process flows, identify any changes or gaps, and discuss what adjustments need to be made for future improvements. It's kind of like spring cleaning, but it happens more frequently and is more structured.

Throughout our day-to-day operations, we log things that are broken or in need of enhancement. These items are then brought to our Management Fix-It meetings where we review potential improvements to our processes. We divide and conquer to tactically make the proposed adjustments, then we come back together to align on the final process. This keeps us organized and efficient and makes our workflow as lean as possible while delivering the highest quality of service to our clients and candidates.

It's an approach that keeps us nimble, agile, and focused on continuous improvement, and that's a mindset every project manager or business founder should adopt. Whether you're working on a small project or overseeing a massive transformation, the ability to step back, evaluate, and refine your process is critical to your long-term success.

PROJECT MANAGEMENT

OUR WHITEBOARD FLOW

One of the most important tools we use for improving our processes is the good old-fashioned whiteboard. In fact, this simple tool not only makes it easier to manage projects, but it also helps us stay on top of important relationships and quickly adjust our strategy to stay on track toward our goals.

We love the visual approach of this tool and the ability to map things out, whether workflows or goals. We'll often make a drawing, and then one of us will come back to the board, erase some parts of that visual, and come up with a new idea or flow that's almost always more efficient.

Every six months or so, we conduct an extensive whiteboard session to review and refine our processes in every area of our businesses, taking a hard look at everything from project workflows to client onboarding processes to internal communication protocols. We do this for both businesses since we're leveraging processes across both fronts. Staying in sync with processes is our secret weapon!

The process we use for these semi-annual whiteboard sessions follows a clear flow:

1 **Review Current Processes:** We start by reviewing what's currently on the whiteboard. That includes our pacing numbers, BHAGs, realistic and minimum revenue targets, lists of pending and active clients, partners, and our Visio process flow. We ask, "What's working well? What isn't?" This gives us a solid foundation to build on.
2 **Identify Gaps and Bottlenecks:** Next, we identify any gaps in our processes or areas where things are slowing down, and we ask ourselves, "Where are we wasting time or resources?" We

also look at where we want to be in the future in terms of our processes so we can explore how to get there.
3. **Brainstorm Solutions:** Next, we sketch out potential solutions to address any gaps. No idea is too big or small at this stage. We put everything out there.
4. **Prioritize Changes:** Once we have a list of ideas, we prioritize them based on their potential impact and ease of implementation. What can we change today? What requires more long-term planning?
5. **Assign Tasks:** Finally, we assign tasks and responsibilities to implement the changes, making sure that each action item has a clear owner and deadline. Anything that isn't identified as a high priority gets placed in our backlog for further consideration at the next whiteboarding session.

Figure 15 is a helpful visual representation of this process. It can help ensure you are regularly streamlining your systems and optimizing their value for you and your clients.

This semi-annual review allows us to maintain lean processes that deliver high-quality service while keeping things simple and efficient. The whiteboard is our constant companion throughout our review as it helps us clearly visualize where we are and where we're going.

Identify & Analyze Current State

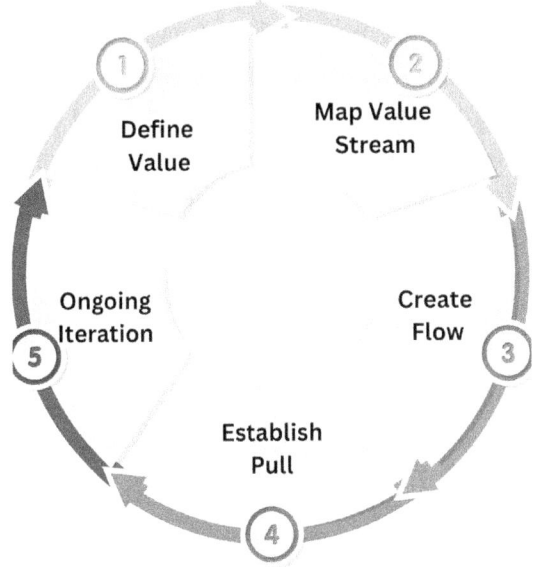

- Map the current workflow and ID any gaps.
- ID activities are are not adding value. Can they be delegated or eliminated?
- Determine the impacts of any changes to the current state process and interconnected flows.
- Iterate on at least a semi-annual basis for improvements.

FIGURE 15

But as much as we love the whiteboard, it's just the first step. Once we've finished our whiteboard session and made decisions about process changes, the next step is to clearly document those processes so they stick. We record everything thoroughly in a standard operating procedure (SOP) document and/or a Loom video (see Figure 16). This creates a reference point that can be shared with team members to ensure consistency and accountability. It also allows us to measure the effectiveness of our changes during the next semi-annual review.

Standard Operating Procedures

- Document the improved process in a workflow view, in a recorded video and in written process documents call SOPs.

- Design these processes for easy expansion for times of growth.

- Test the new process(es) in small iterations to try-test-adjust.

- Plan and train resources to support new or improved processes.

- Regularly update these processes each time you perform a semi-annual process audit/review.

FIGURE 16

PROJECT MANAGEMENT

The whiteboard is a simple (some might even say primitive) tool, but we find that it is incredibly powerful for driving business retrospectives and, ultimately, our success. The act of writing something on the whiteboard makes it real. You can't hide from it. When something is written down, it demands attention and action.

By visualizing the problem, the solution, and the plan, the whiteboard helps us avoid overcomplicating things. We stay focused on what truly matters. And our whiteboard is a living, breathing document that evolves as our business evolves. Whether we're pivoting, scaling, or fine-tuning, it keeps us grounded and adaptable. We also use the whiteboard as part of our five-minute stand-up at the start of every day.

Yes, we realize there are plenty of digital tools and software solutions available, but we find that the simplicity and flexibility of a whiteboard are unmatched. It provides us with the space to brainstorm, strategize, and solve problems in real time, and it keeps us aligned with our long-term vision.

In fact, the whiteboard has been a foundational tool in our business journey. It helped us pivot in the early days, and it now helps us refine our processes as we scale. Whether we're managing a small project or overseeing a large transformation, the whiteboard offers a powerful, flexible way to track our progress, identify areas for improvement, and stay focused on our goals.

So we recommend making the whiteboard your friend. Use it to track your leading and lagging measures, brainstorm new ideas, and visualize the big picture. And most importantly, use it as a tool for constant improvement, whether through daily check-ins or a semi-annual process review.

In project management, clarity and flexibility are of the utmost importance, and a whiteboard is the perfect tool to help you achieve both.

In addition to our whiteboard, we also use a **vision board** to remind ourselves of the big picture. The vision board is a collection of images that we gather and arrange on a poster-sized board to serve as reminders of our various goals. It provides a constant source of inspiration and motivation, so even on the toughest days, we're clear about where we're headed.

The combination of our daily whiteboard check-ins with our long-term vision board keeps us focused on both short-term execution and long-term aspirations. By physically seeing our goals in front of us each and every day, we have constant reminders of the bigger purpose behind each task.

THANK YOU, BUT NO

There are a few other skills we encourage you to master if you want to become an expert at project management (or any professional field). Among these are the ability to clearly and confidently say no to requests. Good project management requires you to set clear expectations and boundaries. As much as you might want to please everyone, saying yes to every request or demand will quickly lead to burnout and a lack of focus on what truly matters.

Saying no often feels uncomfortable, especially in a professional setting where you want to accommodate others. But in reality, no is a complete sentence. It's also a powerful tool that allows you to stay focused on your priorities and avoid overcommitting. Remember, as we've been saying, success is not about how many tasks you can juggle but knowing which projects, clients, and candidates align with your goals and saying no to the ones that don't.

Drawing clear and hard boundaries with clients or colleagues doesn't make you difficult to work with. It makes you effective. By protecting your time and resources, you make sure that the projects you do take on receive your full attention and expertise. So don't be afraid to walk away from projects or situations that compromise your boundaries or values. The short-term discomfort of saying no is far better than the long-term stress of overcommitting.

In fact, saying no is the cornerstone of effective time management. And for those things you say yes to, we recommend using **blocking, batching,** and **prioritization** to ensure they get the time and focus they deserve.

Block, Batch, and Protect

Time blocking is the practice of dedicating specific chunks of time on your calendar to focus on certain tasks without distractions, and as we founders know, context-switching will *kill* productivity and ideation in the fiercest of ways! **Batching** involves grouping similar tasks together so you can knock them out more efficiently. For example, you might block out time each morning for project updates or batch all of your client calls into one afternoon.

Once you block and batch your time, protect those blocks and batches! That means not answering the phone during a deep work period and resisting the urge to respond to every email immediately. During our "hard thinking" block and batch times, we turn off our mobile devices and silence reminders and notifications to allow for better focus.

If you don't protect your time, it becomes really easy for the day to get away from you as your calendar fills up with other people's priorities instead of your own. Without structure, your days become reactive instead of proactive, and you end up scrambling from task to task without any clear direction.

And we've found this lack of structure really increases stress levels as well. Inconsistent time management leads to decreased productivity, missed deadlines, and, ultimately, burnout. So learn to say no, practice blocking and batching, and protect your calendar!

Learn to Negotiate

Finally, remember that saying no and protecting your time doesn't always have to be final. There's an art to negotiation, and sometimes, what starts as a firm boundary can lead to a compromise that works for both parties. Be clear about what you can and cannot do, but remain open to finding solutions that align with both your goals and the client's needs.

Negotiation allows you to maintain your boundaries while still delivering value. For example, if a client requests an unrealistic timeline, rather than simply saying no, you might propose a new deadline that accommodates their needs while protecting your other commitments. The goal is to strike a balance between overpromising and under delivering.

In project management, as in other roles, success often means learning to say no and managing your time effectively but also negotiating wisely. You're not trying to be inflexible but strategic. That way, you can focus on what matters, deliver high-quality work, and maintain a healthy work-life balance.

So protect your boundaries, value your time, and never be afraid to walk away from situations that don't serve your goals. By mastering these skills, you will not only improve your project management but also enhance the quality of your work and relationships.

CONCLUSION

OUR PURPOSE IN WRITING THIS book has been to give you a view into how we got to where we are—from living in and leaving the corporate world to creating two thriving businesses—as well as our leadership philosophy and the valuable lessons we've gathered from both our mistakes and our successes throughout our careers.

Every misstep provided us with a learning opportunity, and each win reaffirmed the strategies that work. By distilling these experiences into actionable insights, we've shared some practical takeaways that you can apply to your own business planning and execution. Whether you are just starting out or you've been in the game for years, we believe that the strategies we've developed can help, especially if you are considering leaving your corporate job to launch your own business.

From our time in the corporate world to our time building and growing multiple businesses, we have tackled a wide range of challenges by creating structure, simplifying processes, and relentlessly pursuing operational improvements. We didn't just inherit polished systems and implement them. We created them by evaluating procedures, identifying gaps, and streamlining processes in order to make them as efficient and effective as possible.

DOUBLING DOWN AS DUALPRENEURS

Running a business of any size is undeniably hard work, and it demands more than just passion. You also need to have discipline, resilience, and a structured approach to manage your time and resources. As we know from personal experience and the experiences of many other business owners, it is easy to get overwhelmed by the sheer volume of tasks and responsibilities. However, with the right framework, you can maintain focus and make real progress, but it must be a structured approach that not only helps you stay organized but carefully divides your time between professional demands and personal commitments.

By leaning into your strengths, clarifying roles and responsibilities within your team, and focusing on making meaningful connections, you will set a strong foundation for your business to thrive. For us, the importance of networking and building relationships can't be overstated. Indeed, many of our most successful client engagements and projects have been a direct result of the connections we've nurtured along the way.

When the right elements are in place, you can not only run your business more effectively but you will also start to enjoy the process. Running a business will become less about survival and more about creating something meaningful and rewarding. And ultimately, if you have a solid, well-thought-out process and you stick to it consistently, you can apply it to almost any area of your life.

In fact, the very same collaborative framework we've outlined throughout this book was the one we used to write it. We didn't just talk about it, we applied it. This book, as much as anything else we've done, is a product of our approach to business.

Finally, if you would like more information about any topic we've covered in this book, or if you just want to make a new professional connection, feel free to reach out to us. You can find us on LinkedIn (https://www.linkedin.com/in/travisjanko/ and https://

CONCLUSION

www.linkedin.com/in/angela-janko/) or email us directly (travis@gsd-coach.com and angela@doneprojectmanagement.com).
We wish you much success in business and in life! Let's go!

ACKNOWLEDGMENTS

We'd like to acknowledge and thank our family, friends, professional network and partners, former leaders, clients, candidates, project teams, and all those who have mentored and encouraged us throughout our careers. "Each One, Teach One" is the gift we have received from these individuals, work tribes, and personal communities, and with this book, we're passing this gift along.

Thank you for believing in us and letting us "try, test, adjust" as we went along. We are also here for your success too!

ABOUT THE AUTHORS

Travis Janko, a veteran sales leader with more than twenty years of experience, transitioned from corporate success to entrepreneurship over eight years ago. He's also a speaker, mentor, and author of *You, of All People: Outrageous Stories & Billion-Dollar Lessons from a SaaS Sales VP Turned 7-Figure Recruiting Agency Founder*.

Angie Janko excels in people, process, and project management. Her genius lies in tackling complex initiatives, creating clear visions, and leveraging individual strengths to solve business challenges.

Travis and Angie also co-lead two businesses, GSD Coach & Recruiting, a sales recruiting agency, and Done! LLC, a project management consulting firm. They reside in Aurora, Colorado, have a family of four children and seven grandchildren, and enjoy traveling, hiking, and cooking together.

ENDNOTES

1 Page, Oliver, "How to Leave Your Comfort Zone and Enter Your 'Growth Zone,'" *Motivation & Goals* (blog), November 4, 2020, https://positivepsychology.com/comfort-zone/.

2 Grenny, Joseph, Kerry Patterson, Ron McMillan, Al Switzler, and Emily Gregory, *Crucial Conversations: Tools for Talking When Stakes Are High*, McGraw Hill, 2021.

3 Thomas, Kenneth W., and Ralph H. Kilmann, *Thomas-Kilmann Conflict Mode Instrument*. Xicom, a subsidiary of CPP, Inc., 1974.

4 Collins, Jim, and Jerry I. Porras, *Built to Last: Successful Habits of Visionary Companies*, Harper Business, 1994.

5 "John Wooden Quotes," BrainyQuote, accessed September 30, 2024, https://www.brainyquote.com/quotes/john_wooden_402561.

6 "Winston Churchill Quotes," BrainyQuote, accessed September 30, 2024, https://www.brainyquote.com/quotes/winston_churchill_131188.

7 "Josh McDowell Quotes," QuoteFancy, accessed September 30, 2024, https://quotefancy.com/quote/1319323/Josh-McDowell-It-is-more-rewarding-to-resolve-a-conflict-than-to-dissolve-a-relationship.

8 Parker, Sam, *212° the Extra Degree: How to Achieve Results Beyond Your Wildest Expectations*, Walk the Talk, 2022.

DOUBLING DOWN AS DUALPRENEURS

9   "Motivational Quotes," QuoteFancy, accessed September 30, 2024, https://quotefancy.com/quote/1707964/Bob-Proctor-What-you-think-about-you-bring-about.

10   "Elbert Hubbard Quotes," BrainyQuote, accessed September 30, 2024, https://www.brainyquote.com/quotes/elbert_hubbard_138643.